HALO
DISASTER RESPONSE DOG

Text by
STEPHANIE PETERS

Little, Brown and Company
New York Boston

Copyright © 2019 by Cosmic Picture Limited

Interior photographs on pages 38–46: Belgian Malinois © Ekaterina Brusnika/Shutterstock.com; bloodhound © Kuznetsov Alexey/Shutterstock.com; border collie © Lobstrosity/Shutterstock.com; German shepherd © Osetrik/Shutterstock.com; golden retriever © Lunja/Shutterstock.com; Labrador retriever © Gerald Marella/Shutterstock.com; Newfoundland © Waldemar Dabrowski/Shutterstock.com; Saint Bernard © rokopix/Shutterstock.com; Siberian husky © Aleksandr Abrosimov/Shutterstock.com

Diagram on page 100 used courtesy of FEMA/FEMA News Photo

Photographs on insert pages 1, 3 (top), and 4 copyright © 2019 by Bernardo Nogueira, for Cosmic Picture Limited. Photographs on insert pages 2, 3 (bottom), 5, 6, and 7 copyright © 2019 by Danny Wilcox Frazier VII, for Cosmic Picture Limited. Photograph on insert p. 8 copyright © 2019 by Cosmic Picture Limited.

Front Cover Key Art and Title Treatment copyright © 2019 by Cosmic Picture Limited. Photo of sky © GlebSStock/Shutterstock.com. Photo of rubble © Georgi Nutsov/Shutterstock.com. Photo of flare © kagankiris/Shutterstock.com. IMAX® is registered trademark of IMAX Corporation. Cover design by Neil Swaab. Cover copyright © 2019 by Hachette Book Group, Inc.

Hachette Book Group supports the right to free expression and the value of copyright. The purpose of copyright is to encourage writers and artists to produce the creative works that enrich our culture.

The scanning, uploading, and distribution of this book without permission is a theft of the author's intellectual property. If you would like permission to use material from the book (other than for review purposes), please contact permissions@hbgusa.com. Thank you for your support of the author's rights.

Little, Brown and Company
Hachette Book Group
1290 Avenue of the Americas, New York, NY 10104
Visit us at LBYR.com

First Edition: March 2019

Little, Brown and Company is a division of Hachette Book Group, Inc. The Little, Brown name and logo are trademarks of Hachette Book Group, Inc.

The publisher is not responsible for websites (or their content) that are not owned by the publisher.

Library of Congress Control Number: 2018957882

ISBNs: 978-0-316-45363-9 (pbk.), 978-0-316-45365-3 (ebook)

Printed in the United States of America

LSC-C

10 9 8 7 6 5 4 3 2 1

SUPERPOWER DOGS

HALO

DISASTER RESPONSE DOG

Halo dangled high above a vast sea of smoldering wreckage. Strapped in a forward-facing harness that held her against the front of her human partner's body, she could see and smell and even feel the disaster that consumed the area below and beyond. Thick black smoke from a nearby fire hit her sensitive nostrils. Her amber eyes darted over the cracked concrete blocks and bricks, the shattered glass and jagged debris. Dust from the debris blew up on a sudden gust of wind, clouding her vision, before settling into her mottled brown-black fur.

In the wild, primal instinct would have told her to flee. But Halo remained calm. More than two years of intensive training had prepared her for this.

"Here we go, girl."

Halo's ears pricked into sharp furry points at the sound of Captain Kristian Labrada's voice. Sandy-haired and strong, both in spirit and in body, Cat was Halo's trainer, her handler, her friend. She had been Halo's constant companion from the moment Cat had chosen her, the runt of the litter, over the other available Dutch shepherd puppies. Their bond was unbreakable, their trust and love for each other absolute.

Cat shifted in her harness and adjusted the line anchored to the building rooftop. Halo's own harness was attached to Cat's, and when Cat moved, Halo swayed with her, gently bumping her sturdy canine body against her trainer's muscular legs.

"Here we go," Cat repeated. She loosened her grip on the line, and together, they slowly rappelled off the last remaining intact building.

Halo tensed as they neared the wreckage. Buried somewhere in the crumbling acres of rubble was a person clinging to life. She had to find that person... before it was too late.

They reached the end of the line. Her paws and

Cat's feet touched down, and Cat unclipped Halo's harness, then her own. Nose twitching, Halo filtered through a mixture of odors, some overpowering, some faint, as she waited for Cat's command.

Cat knelt behind her and gave her back a tap. "Ready?" Halo gave a short bark. "Search!"

With that one word, Halo's training kicked in. She left Cat's side and made her way down into the depths of the concrete jungle. She paced out a zigzag pattern as her keen sense of smell picked up one scent after another—oil-filmed water, rotting garbage, rodent droppings—in rapid-fire succession. The odors were tantalizing, beckoning her to follow them. But Halo resisted. None were what she'd been trained to track. That all-important smell still eluded her.

She widened her scope, stepping delicately around and over shards of broken glass, tangles of twisted wires, and deadly spears of rusted metal. The shell of a wrecked car gave off the promising scent of human, but after pausing for a second whiff of the air, Halo moved on. The scent was too faint and too cold to be the human she was looking for.

As she searched, the shadows cast by the collapsed

buildings and mountains of debris lengthened. The sun would soon be setting, plunging the disaster site into darkness. Time was running out.

Halo trotted on, back and forth. Suddenly, her nostril receptors lit up like a pinball machine. She'd passed through a scent cone—an invisible cloud of odor coming off the victim. If visible, the cloud would have been roughly the shape of an ice-cream cone. The scent was most intense at the cone's point, where the victim was, and much fainter and spread out at the cone's open end. Halo had walked somewhere in the middle. She checked her stride, backed up a step, and sniffed the air again. *Yes*, her brain cried out. *This is it.*

Quivering with excitement, Halo began circling, zeroing in on the odor's source. The area was strewn with dangers—overhangs that could collapse without warning, shifting rubble that might avalanche beneath her paws, water-slick planks that would send her sliding off into emptiness. So, nose hoovering up the scent, Halo moved with cautious haste. Past the skeletal remains of a building, around a deep sinkhole partially filled with stagnant water, and down a length of old railroad track to a mangled train car flipped on its side.

Yes. The smell was strongest here. Overpowering, even. She hesitated for a moment, moved away, and sniffed again.

No. The scent wasn't as intense here.

Doubt vanished. Halo darted back to her previous spot and gave three sharp barks. *Here! Hurry! Hurry!*

Something was up. The puppy sensed it the moment her humans, Jason and Sara, came into the room. Excitement and nervousness clung to them as heavily as the smell of their breakfasts.

She licked her chops. *Mmm. Breakfast.* Now it was her turn to eat. She snuffled at Jason as he filled her food bowl, then dove into the kibble with intent focus. That done, she followed him to the door, where Sara waited with a pink collar and lead.

"Let's go, girl," she said.

A gust of frigid winter air and wet snowflakes blasted them all in the face when Jason opened the door. Sara muttered with annoyance, but the puppy wriggled with excitement. She loved snow. Playing in it, rolling in it, burrowing in it, peeing in it. It was all good.

No playtime now, though. Jason let her turn a patch of snow yellow, then he popped the hatch of his SUV, picked her up, and put her into the travel crate there. "Well, Pink," he said, ruffling her soft pointed ears. "I hope you like traveling because if things work out today, you're going on a long trip." The puppy didn't understand a word, but Jason's warm tone and affectionate touch set her whiplike tail thumping.

The thrum of the engine vibrated up through the puppy's body when Jason started the car. She stood and tried to look out the car window from her crate, but the vehicle bounced her off balance. So she turned three times, lay down with her head on her paws, gave a breathy *whuff*, and dozed off.

She awoke when the car stopped and her crate opened. "Come on, girl," Sara encouraged.

She didn't need a second invitation. There was snow here, too, blowing and swirling about in thick waves across an ice-encrusted parking lot. Sara and Jason waited patiently while she marked a drift, but when she tried to chase after some flakes, Sara gently tugged her lead in the opposite direction. "No time for that. Got a surprise for you."

Her humans led her into a big white building and let her off the lead. Inside was a wide-open space with chairs and couches and tall plants arranged around the perimeter. Sitting on one of the couches was a man she knew well: Nick, the breeder, whose home she had lived in for weeks before Jason and Sara brought her to their house. Next to him was a woman who smelled vaguely familiar. The puppy took three steps toward them—and froze, nostrils twitching furiously. She'd caught the scent of someone she knew well. *Two* someones. When she heard a little yip, she took off running, toenails clicking on the white tiled floor. She skittered around the far couch and ran smack into two other puppies. Her sisters!

She and her sisters came from the same litter of eleven Dutch shepherd puppies, eight girls and three boys. They'd all lived together with their mother after they were born. Then one by one, her siblings left with humans. First a sweet-tempered sister who used to lick her ears when they snuggled together. Then a burly oaf who roughhoused too aggressively and stole the best toys. When only three girls were left, a woman—*Ahh! That's who the woman on the couch is!*—had taken one of the sisters to foster and socialize. The other stayed with Nick, and she had gone with Jason and Sara.

But now, the three girls were together again, one sister wearing a teal collar, the other an orange one, and she herself in pink. She bounced on her front paws, circling around them with happy barks. Teal flinched. A skittish thing, she'd always shied away from wrestling matches and balked at loud noises. Orange responded with a throaty woof and a playful pounce, and then promptly piddled on the floor.

Nick had been grinning at their reunion. Now he groaned. "Really?"

Shamed, Orange flattened her ears. Pink's own ears stayed up in pointed triangles. She may have been the littlest in the litter, the runt, but she didn't make puddles inside. Not anymore, at least.

Nick cleaned up the mess, then sat back on his haunches and looked at his phone. "There's someone special on her way to meet you guys," he announced after reading a text. "A woman named Cat." He chuckled. "A woman named Cat who works with dogs. You can't make this stuff up."

Cat narrowed her eyes at the wintry whiteout beyond her car windshield. One part of her brain was thinking how nice it would be to be back in sunny Miami instead of here in snowy Detroit. Another part was cataloging the different accidents that could happen under these blizzard-like conditions. A spinout on black ice. A skid off the road. Rear-ended by another car. The possibilities were endless. Fortunately, she wasn't driving far. Besides, if anybody knew what to do in an accident, it was her, Captain Kristian Labrada of the Miami-Dade Fire Rescue (MDFR) Department.

She yawned. Yesterday's plane ride and a bad night's sleep at an airport hotel were catching up with her. She was used to working on little sleep. Still—

"Whoever invented coffee should get a medal," she murmured. She reached for the steaming cup in the holder beside her. As she did, she glimpsed the red, white, and blue arm patch on her jacket. *U.S. Department of Homeland Security*, it read. *National US&R Response System.*

In addition to her job with the MDFR, Cat worked

for FEMA, the Federal Emergency Management Agency. Specifically, she was a canine trainer and handler for Florida Task Force 1—or FL-TF1—one of FEMA's twenty-eight elite Urban Search and Rescue teams. That role was what brought her to Detroit: to choose a new puppy to train for the canine task force, a top-notch group of dogs and human partners who deployed to cities destroyed by disasters to search for missing people.

She finished her coffee in one gulp and pulled into the lot of the car dealership where she was scheduled to meet a breeder named Nick. Sure enough, a man emerged from the big white building and waved at her. Tugging her knit cap more snugly over her blonde hair, Cat got out of her car.

"So, Cat, you ready to see the pups?" the man said after they shook hands.

Cat blew on her bare fingertips and nodded. But as she followed Nick into the building, she wondered, *Am I ready?*

Cat had trained three other dogs in the eighteen years she'd been with the Florida Task Force. All had been female yellow Labrador retrievers. Like most people, Cat was drawn to their liquid brown eyes, smiling mouths, and playful nature. But more than that, she appreciated their intelligence, their loyalty, their bravery, and their strength. Those traits made them dream dogs to work with, especially the females, who in her experience learned faster—and peed on everything less—than the males. Cat had trusted her Labs, believed in their abilities. They weren't just dogs or pets to her; they were her partners. And to the people they located who were in serious trouble, they were something even more. They were heroes.

Siren was supposed to be one of those heroes.

A sudden lump lodged in Cat's throat. Siren was her last dog. For two years, Cat had trained her for search and rescue missions. Siren was getting ready to test for her FEMA certification. If she passed—and there was no doubt in Cat's mind that she would—they would be ready to deploy to their first disaster together.

But then without warning, Siren got sick. Kidney failure, the veterinarians told her. Nothing they did made a difference. The once-energetic two-and-a-half-year-old suddenly looked and moved like a dog ten times her age. And then, three months ago…she died.

Cat had lost dogs before. In her childhood, when

her mother had kept Siberian huskies and later, Dobermans. And then Fancy, the first Lab she'd trained for FEMA. Bella, the dog after Fancy, still lived with Cat and her family, but sadly, her mind and body had slowed with age. Siren, the third yellow Lab, would have taken Bella's place.

Cat would never forget Siren or her other dogs, not in a million years. But now was not the time for grief. She needed to focus on why she was in Detroit.

"Yeah," she replied to Nick's question. "I'm ready."

SUPERPOWER DOGS WORLDWIDE

Of all the animals in the world, dogs are our best and most natural allies in times of need. Our bond traces back to prehistory, when their canine ancestors first joined our human ones on hunts in exchange for scraps of meat and a warm fireside bed. Dogs still hunt with us today, but their role in our lives has greatly expanded since those ancient times. Working dogs herd sheep and cattle and guard our homes. Sniffer dogs detect hidden roadside bombs and illegal drugs, and K9 police dogs help nab criminals. Therapy dogs soothe and comfort emotionally troubled people, and service dogs assist those with physical challenges such as blindness, hearing loss, and other disabilities.

And then there are the search and rescue dogs. These canines undergo two years of rigorous training to be certified for one purpose: to locate and save humans in serious trouble. Sometimes it's just one or two people. A missing child lost in an overgrown wilderness, a worker trapped beneath a collapsed building, a hiker injured after a fall down a mountainside, a skier buried beneath an avalanche—the list of individuals who owe their lives to rescue dogs goes on and on.

But too often, these brave dogs and their human partners are deployed to catastrophic events that have taken the lives of thousands and threaten thousands more. Canines and their handlers arrived in New York City within hours of the horrific terrorist attacks on the World Trade Center in 2001. They went to New Orleans in 2005 after Hurricane Katrina and, twelve years later, to Texas, Florida, and Puerto Rico after Hurricanes Harvey, Irma, and Maria. They flew to Haiti in 2010, when a devastating earthquake and its aftershocks killed hundreds of thousands, and to Turkey in 2011, when a similarly powerful quake destroyed areas of the country. In these disasters and others—too many others—search and rescue dogs from all over the globe climbed over and around wreckage, dug into rubble, forged through water-soaked ruins, and tunneled beneath piles of teetering debris, risking their own safety for the sake of human lives.

They are truly Superpower Dogs.

Pink growled low in her throat. She had been happily mouthing a squeaky stuffed animal chew toy when Orange sneaked up and tried to steal it. Now, their rumps high and teeth sunk deep into either end of the soggy toy, they were in a ferocious tug-of-war. Pink did not intend to lose, but her sister's bigger size wasn't making victory easy. With every backward pull Orange made, Pink skidded forward a few inches.

A door opened and closed behind her. Pink recognized Nick's scent. There was someone with him—a woman, judging by her voice and smell. The puppy was curious about the newcomer. But she stayed focused on winning back her toy.

Orange's eyes shifted, though. And her grip loosened slightly.

Pink felt the change. She gave a mighty yank, twisting her head to the side at the same time. The toy flew out of Orange's mouth. They both lost their balance and took a few staggering steps. Pink righted herself first and scrambled away behind the couch, madly squeaking her prize the whole way.

Nick, the newcomer, and the other humans burst out laughing. "That little one's got nerve," the newcomer commented.

"Oh yeah," Nick agreed. "She may be small, but she's no pushover. Seems smart, too."

The couch cushions creaked. "Hey there."

Pink stopped mouthing the toy and looked up. The newcomer was peering over the edge at her. Her medium-length blonde hair was caught in a ponytail at the back of her head, except for one stray lock that fell across her forehead. Her hazel eyes tilted up at the corners. When she smiled, those corners crinkled. Her breath smelled of coffee.

"Can I play, too?" Pink watched warily as the woman slowly reached down toward the chew toy.

Just before the woman's fingers connected with the drool-wet fabric, the puppy jumped up and dashed away.

But not *too* far away. Pink flopped on a piece of mat, gnawing on the toy to make it squeak, while sneaking glances at the blonde woman who now sat on the edge of the couch. The warm richness of her voice, her keen and probing looks, her smell of snow and deodorant and coffee, the energy of her movements—everything about the newcomer fascinated the puppy. So, when the woman called to her, she abandoned the toy and trotted over.

She doesn't move like Siren or Bella.

That was Cat's first thought when the puppy padded toward her. Then she rolled her eyes at herself. *Duh. Of course she doesn't. She's a Dutch shepherd, not a yellow Lab. Different body shape, different gait.*

When the puppy was close enough, Cat eased her hand toward her muzzle. The dog drew back. Cat stopped, hand outstretched. The little shepherd regarded her for a moment, then leaned forward and sniffed her fingers. Cat waited a beat before she curled her palm over the puppy's ears. When the dog didn't run off, she began stroking her head.

Everything about her is so different, Cat thought. Instead of an even coat of blonde fur, the puppy was covered with muddled black and brown bands, a coloring pattern known as brindle. All her Labs had had warm brown eyes. This puppy's eyes reminded her of coal and amber—a pure black pupil surrounded by an orange-brown iris. Her muzzle was more pointed and her face more streamlined than any yellow Lab's, and her ears perked up into neat triangles instead of hanging in floppy folds. And yet…

Cat captured one of the puppy's ears and gently rubbed its silky softness between her thumb and forefinger. When the puppy's eyes glazed, Cat smiled. "So, you like a good ear rub, huh?" she murmured. "My other dogs did, too."

After a moment, though, she let go and straightened. She wasn't there to pet the puppies. She was there to observe and evaluate them. If she'd been alone, she would have run through her tests on her own. But since the dogs' foster parents were there—

"Can you guys help me see how the puppies act when I throw some stuff around them?"

Nick shrugged. "Sure. What do you need us to do?"

"Just play with them like you normally would." Cat rose from the couch with a half-full water bottle in hand. "Don't pay any attention to me."

She backed off and watched the puppies playing with their humans. Orange and Teal lost all interest in her. But the little runt with the pink collar kept one eye on her at all times. When Cat skirted the edge of the room, Pink's gaze tracked her, even as she wrestled with Nick over her rag toy.

Good, Cat thought. *But let's see what you do now.*

Without warning, she hurled her water bottle to a far corner. *Whump!* The plastic container ricocheted off the wall and rolled to a stop, its contents sloshing.

"Yikes!" Sara cried in alarm.

The puppies were just as startled. Teal cowered in fear. Orange ran away and dribbled pee at the same time. Pink dropped her toy and darted away, too. But moments later, she came trotting back. Her body language practically screamed, *What the heck was that?*

Cat smiled. Curiosity was vital in rescue dogs.

Without it, they'd never venture into unknown territory. "Okay. Let's see if that's a one-time thing, or if you're always sniffing around to see what's up."

Slowly, she picked up a small metal wastebasket and threw it. *Crash!* Once again, the puppies scattered, though this time none of them peed. And once again, only little Pink hurried back to see what all the commotion was about.

"What, exactly, was the point of that?" Jason asked.

"I'm watching to see how they react to distractions," Cat answered, snapping her fingers at Pink, who shrank back for a second before returning. "And to see if they can recover quickly. Or if they act like that." She jerked her chin at Teal, who was staying as far away from her as the room allowed. "I need to know they're curious, too. Dogs who aren't curious or can't recover after being distracted don't have a prayer of making it through the training or passing the certification tests."

"Have you ever ended up with a dog that didn't pass?" Sara asked.

"Never," Cat replied. She flipped over a nearby plastic bin and drummed on it. She watched Pink and watched Pink watching her. "I go with my gut feeling," she added. "It's how I've always chosen my puppies."

"So, what is your gut telling you about these three?" Nick wanted to know.

Cat didn't respond immediately. Instead, she picked up the drool-wet squeaker toy by the tail and waved it enticingly at Pink. The little Dutch shepherd hesitated, but only for a second, before darting forward and grabbing the other end. *Squeak! Squeak! Squeak!*

Cat smiled. "My gut is telling me that this little girl has what I'm looking for."

Nick nodded. "That's the one I'd have chosen, too. I mean, all three come from good stock, what with their mom being an agility champion and their dad working as a police dog. But of all the pups, males included, she's the one who takes after her parents the most."

Cat appreciated Nick's input, but it was the puppy herself who had convinced her, not her parentage. She knelt down and held out the pink lead. With a trusting little yip, the runt trotted over, tail wagging and tongue lolling.

The pup's eagerness brought a sudden tear to Cat's

eye. She wiped it away, fixed the lead to the little Dutch shepherd's pink collar, and scooped her up. "Yeah. She's the one. I even have a name for her." She buried her nose in the puppy's fur.

"Halo. Her name is Halo."

CAT AND HER DOGS

Before Cat became a dog handler and a member of the Miami-Dade Fire Rescue, she lived and worked in Orlando from 1992 to 1999 as a marine mammal trainer. But after seven years, she decided it was time to try something new. She moved back to her hometown of Miami and got a job working in a veterinary clinic. And she decided something else, too: she was going to get a dog.

Fancy, a beautiful yellow Labrador retriever, came to live with Cat in 1999. Cat chose her from the litter after the pup escaped her dog pen. "That told me she was smart," Cat remembers. "And I wanted a smart dog."

Fancy's mother had been a show dog, and for a short time, Cat considered entering Fancy into dog shows, too. But that idea went out the window when a woman wearing a Miami-Dade Urban Search and Rescue—or US&R—T-shirt came into the veterinary clinic. Something clicked for Cat when she saw that shirt. Instead of a show dog, she began training Fancy to become a search and rescue dog.

Cat and Fancy embarked on the unknown journey together. "I was a civilian then. I'd never trained a dog that way before," Cat recalls. Still, she had a degree in zoology, the study of animal behavior and physiology, and she understood that dogs needed motivation to work hard. She knew exactly what motivated Fancy: food. Together, they both got certified in 2002, Cat as a dog handler and Fancy as her search and rescue dog. And together, they deployed to several disasters—Hurricanes Charley, Frances, Ivan, and Jeanne in 2004, Dennis and Katrina in 2005, and a Barbados apartment building collapse in 2007—until a problem with Fancy's lungs forced Cat to retire her. And then, when Fancy's suffering became too great, Cat was compelled to say a final good-bye to her brave dog.

Cat grieved for Fancy, but she wasn't ready to give up her role as a search and rescue dog handler. She adopted and trained another yellow Lab, named Bella.

"She was my rock star," Cat says of her second dog,

who was certified the summer of 2007. Everything about their partnership worked. It was almost as if Bella could read her mind at times.

But then, something changed. Bella began clinging to Cat as if she was afraid to leave her side. She seemed to sense something about Cat. Something bad. Bella's instincts were right. Cat had cancer. Cat was treated and made it through. But Bella never quite snapped back to her former self, and Cat retired her to live out her days as the family's beloved pet.

Once more, Cat set out to find a yellow Lab to train. A breeder sent her a sweet little dog who Cat named Siren. But within a few weeks, Cat realized something was wrong with Siren's knee. Much as she liked the pup, a dog with a bad knee would never be a search and rescue dog. So she sent her back to the breeder and accepted another puppy from the same litter. She called this one Siren as well, and together, they plunged into two years of arduous training. Siren was on the brink of receiving her certification in 2015 when, out of nowhere, she became sick. The diagnosis was kidney failure. There was no cure. Siren passed away within weeks of her diagnosis.

And now, there was Halo, Cat's fourth dog. She'd have big pawsteps to follow after Fancy, Bella, and Siren…but with Cat at her side, she'd have every chance in the world of success.

Halo had a belly full of kibble and was ready to romp. She just needed someone to romp with. Her first choice was Bella, the old yellow Lab who lived in her new home. But when she hurried over to the couch where Bella lay, the older dog just lifted her head, looked at her for a second, and flopped back down. Rejected but not undeterred, Halo ran two quick circles around the couch, then tore out of the grand room in search of another playmate.

Two weeks had passed since Halo got off the plane in Miami with Cat. Her world was completely different now. Gone were the snow and cold winds and icy bare ground. Instead, there was heat and humidity and green grass begging to be marked. There was a cozy kennel in one corner of the bedroom Cat shared with her husband, Pete, and kibble three times a day. There was the human boy named Lance who slept in another bedroom and whose school backpack sometimes held tasty food that—sadly—wasn't for her. There was Bella, of course, who never wanted to play. And there was Rugger, the big fluffy black Manx cat, who sometimes did.

That's who Halo went in search of now.

Rugger was stretched out in a patch of sunshine on the floor when Halo barreled up beside him. The cat sprang to his feet, ready to fend off the attack. Halo danced in a circle around him, panting and yipping and tail-wagging furiously. Rugger matched her movements, never turning his back to the puppy, before making his escape to a nearby chair.

Halo pursued and, with a happy bark, darted in to try to mouth the cat's neck. Rugger defended himself with a well-placed swipe of his paw. Back and forth they went, dart and swipe, dart and swipe, until with a hiss that warned, "I've had enough of this," Rugger slashed a claw across Halo's sensitive snout.

Halo backed away, looking more surprised than hurt. Ears back, Rugger glared at her from his chair as if defying her to try again. Halo licked her chops and shifted from paw to paw. Rugger continued glaring. Halo gave up and went in search of a chew toy to maul.

Her toys came from a nearby pet store, one of the places she went with Cat. There were always treats involved on these trips, where sometimes she rode in the cart and sometimes she walked at the end of her pink lead. She met other dogs in that store. The bigger ones let her circle behind them for a quick get-to-know-you whiff. Not the tiny, yappy ones, though. They were usually in their owners' arms, in baskets, or even tucked inside sparkly purses.

She went many other places with Cat, too, like parks and the lake and other people's houses. She hung out at the fire station where both Cat and Pete worked. Her first visit there had been a little frightening, what with the noise and the strangers and the huge trucks that loomed over her. But curiosity conquered fear, and now she moved about the space with confidence.

She spent lots of time at home. That was where she chewed up cardboard paper towel tubes and chased balls and jumped for the colorful soap bubbles Lance blew in the air in the backyard and tore apart soft chew toys—except for her "baby," a stuffed bear that she handled with extra care. She learned how to get in and out of the house by pushing through a screen door and went for runs with Pete. And when errands and playtime were over, and she'd peed in the grass and her kibble bowl was empty, she stretched out on a sunny patch of rug—not Rugger's spot, a different one—and dozed until she heard Cat say that one special word: *Halo*.

"Halo?"

Cat wandered from the kitchen to the front hallway, where her Dutch shepherd puppy had conked out. It had been a busy morning for both of them. First a trip to Lance's school, then a visit to the fire station, and finally a stop at the big-box hardware store. People's reactions at seeing Halo riding in the bright orange cart had varied from gushing and cooing, to doing a surprised double take, to drawing back in alarm. She understood that last response. Halo was adorable, as all puppies were, but with her sharp teeth, pointed muzzle, dark fur, and intense amber and black eyes, she could look a little intimidating. It was no fault of her own; those were simply the physical traits of her breed. Halo's personality was certainly not vicious. But Cat recognized that unlike her yellow Labs, who had been all floppy limbs and big feet and soulful eyes at this age, her Dutch shepherd puppy seemed poised for action, like a frog ready to snatch a fly with its lightning-quick tongue.

Well, *sometimes* she seemed poised for action, anyway. "Silly dog," Cat murmured affectionately as she ruffled the sleepy pup's ears. "What do you say we have a little playtime in the backyard? Huh, Halo?"

Cat emphasized the name just a little and smiled, pleased, when the puppy flicked open her eyes and got to her feet. As a search and rescue dog candidate, it was vital Halo responded quickly when Cat said her name. She'd need to understand that Cat was talking to *her*, that when they were on a rescue, the commands Cat was giving were for *her*. That's why, for the past two weeks, Cat had been rewarding Halo with treats whenever she came when called.

She'd also been working on an important command: *Leave it!* Those two words were preferable to *No!*, which sounded too much like other words and could confuse a dog. With *Leave it!* the meaning was never in doubt, especially when issued in a firm, no-nonsense tone. The command delivered the same basic message—*stop doing what you're doing*—but could be used in countless situations. Cat had been tempted to test out Halo's response to it earlier, when the puppy was pestering Rugger. But she knew the old Manx cat could protect himself. And besides, Halo had likely learned another valuable lesson: leave Rugger alone when he was hissing and swiping.

"Hey, girl, how about some jump time?"

Halo began wriggling with excitement. Not from the question. Cat knew she wouldn't recognize any of those words. But just as Halo was learning to associate the strict tone of *Leave it!* with a certain expected behavior, she was also figuring out that Cat's playful tone meant fun.

Outside in the fenced-in backyard, Cat boosted Halo onto a small enclosed trampoline, then climbed in beside her. To a casual observer, it probably looked like they were goofing around. But there was a very real purpose to the trampoline time. Out in the field, Halo would be expected to walk, run, and climb over uneven, shifting terrain. The trampoline was a good way to simulate that experience with her three-and-a-half-month-old pup.

Eyes on Halo, Cat started bouncing on both feet at the same time. Small motions at first, just enough to make the trampoline wobble under Halo's paws. Would the pup lose her balance and topple over, or would she adjust her stance to compensate for the unsteady surface?

Halo adjusted.

"Good girl!" Cat praised warmly. She pulled one of Halo's toys from her back pocket and let her take hold of it with her teeth. Then she bounced a little higher, making the surface more difficult to stand on. Halo moved seamlessly with the motion, rarely tripping or stumbling even after Cat added a few small balls and chew toys and changed her two-footed bounce to a rapid one-two, one-two march.

When the session ended, Cat was hot and sweaty but happy. Halo had performed like a champ. Now she deserved a good cooldown in the plastic wading pool. Cat laughed as Halo frolicked and splashed while Cat sprayed her with the hose.

Pete drove up during the cooldown. "Looks like today went well!"

"Oh yeah." Cat jiggled the hose so that fat water droplets cascaded on and around Halo. "She's doing great on the trampoline and being around new people and loud, busy places. In fact, it's time to kick it up a notch." She grinned as Halo leaped to snap at the water stream. "Next week, Halo and I are going to the US&R site."

SUPERPOWER DOG BREEDS

Loyal, intelligent, curious, agile, and eager to work. It's these qualities, plus their keen senses, that make Dutch shepherds like Halo ideal search and rescue dogs. But they're just one of many breeds that are consistently found doing this important work. Turn the page to discover some of the others that make the grade.

BELGIAN MALINOIS

Appearance: Lean and muscular, medium build, with a short brown coat, a plume tail, pointed black ears, dark eyes, and black muzzle

Temperament: Intelligent, friendly, energetic, hardworking

Superpower: Easy to train because they love working, especially when treats are involved.

Ideal jobs: Search and rescue; service

Fun fact: Malinois have been used by the Secret Service to patrol the grounds of the White House.

BLOODHOUND

Appearance: A big, muscular dog with extra-long ears that hang past drooping jowls; mostly brown with some black on the ears, back, and muzzle; a straight, whiplike tail; black-brown soulful eyes

Temperament: Inquisitive, patient, relentless, friendly

Superpower: The top dogs in scent detection, they won't give up their pursuit until they find their target.

Ideal job: Tracking criminals and lost or missing people

Fun fact: A pair of bloodhounds named Tipper and Tony have helped catch illegal rhino and elephant poachers in Kenya.

BORDER COLLIE

Appearance: Medium build with a thick coat that is either straight or wavy, in a variety of shades of black, white, gray, and brown; expressive ears can perk up or sit flat; the eyes can be blue, black, or brown

Temperament: Focused, highly intelligent, energetic

Superpowers: Bred for herding sheep, the border collie is incredibly agile and an expert at scenting the air.

Ideal job: Search and rescue

Fun fact: A border collie named Striker made it into the Guinness World Records in the category "Fastest Car Window Opened by a Dog" with a time of 11.34 seconds.

GERMAN SHEPHERD

Appearance: Medium build, muscular, lean, and athletic, with a thick coat of two-tone fur in shades of brown and black; black eyes, long muzzle, pointed triangular ears, and a bushy tail

Temperament: Loyal, courageous, confident, hardworking, highly intelligent

Superpowers: Fearless fighters and extremely trainable, they make ideal police and guard dogs.

Ideal jobs: Search and rescue; service

Fun fact: A New York City police German shepherd named Appollo was awarded the Dickin Medal, the highest accolade an animal can receive, for his bravery during search and rescue missions after the September 11 terrorist attacks.

GOLDEN RETRIEVER

Appearance: A medium-size dog with long, wavy, blond fur, soulful dark eyes, a broad head, and floppy ears that hang down by its smiling mouth; a long plume of a tail

Temperament: Friendly, obedient, playful, smart, outgoing, loyal

Superpowers: Good hunting dogs, excellent swimmers, great companions—but lousy guard dogs. They're too friendly!

Ideal jobs: Search and rescue; emotional therapy; service

Fun fact: One of the most popular breeds, golden retrievers have been featured in television shows and commercials, lived in the White House, and found fame on the internet.

LABRADOR RETRIEVER

Appearance: A sturdy, medium-size dog with a short dense coat of yellow, chocolate, or black fur; wide head, expressive eyes, and a long, tapered "otter" tail that seems to never stop wagging!

Temperament: Friendly, obedient, playful, easygoing, smart

Superpower: Originally bred for retrieving water fowl and accompanying fishermen, Labs are top-notch swimmers.

Ideal jobs: Search and rescue; emotional therapy; service

Fun fact: The Labrador originally came from Newfoundland, not Labrador!

NEWFOUNDLAND

Appearance: An enormous, powerful dog with extremely thick fur; its coat can be combinations of black, brown, gray, and white; broad head, floppy ears, drool-drenched muzzle, and deep brown eyes

Temperament: Sweet tempered, loyal, gentle

Superpowers: Commonly used to accompany fishermen and seafarers on board ships, they have partially webbed feet that make them exceptionally strong swimmers, and their super strength allows them to save drowning people and even tow many to safety at once.

Ideal job: Water rescue

Fun fact: A Newfie named Seaman accompanied Meriwether Lewis and William Clark on their 1804 expedition to explore the western United States.

SIBERIAN HUSKY

Appearance: An athletic, medium-size dog with a thick fur coat that ranges from all white to white and brown to white, gray, and black; almond-shaped eyes that are blue or brown—sometimes one of each!—triangular pointed ears, long bushy tail, triangular head

Temperament: Loyal, friendly, outgoing, highly intelligent

Superpowers: Bred for pulling sleds across the Arctic tundra, Siberian huskies have incredible endurance and speed, and they can withstand subzero temperatures for long periods of time.

Ideal job: Search and rescue, particularly avalanche recovery

Fun fact: In 1925, a Siberian husky named Balto helped deliver lifesaving serum through a blizzard to residents of Nome, Alaska. A statue in his honor stands in Central Park in New York City.

HONORABLE MENTION

SAINT BERNARD

Appearance: A very large, muscular dog with ponderous jowls, a broad nose, a wrinkly forehead, and floppy ears; short fur in a variety of shades of red, brown, black, and white; distinct mask of black or brown on its face; drools a lot!

Temperament: Patient, calm, loyal

Superpower: Strong enough to pull small carts

Ideal job: Once a search and rescue breed, now primarily a family companion

Fun fact: Barry the Saint Bernard was the original poster dog of snowy rescues. From 1800 to 1812, he rescued more than forty people from a treacherous mountain pass in the Swiss Alps.

Of all the places Cat had taken her, this was the most exciting by far. Acres of room to run, huge piles of stuff to climb, and other dogs and people. There was so much to take in—Halo had been a little overwhelmed when they first drove up. But now, out of her kennel and surrounded by the intriguing sights, sounds, and smells, she was raring to explore.

But exploring was not in the cards. Not unless Cat let her off her lead, anyway—which she didn't.

"So, this is your new trainee?" A dark-haired man with a deep tan crouched in front of Halo. Dangling from his hands were a few tug toys—a rope knotted at both ends, a skinny cloth animal with loops at its head and tail, a wing-shaped double oval made of hard plastic. "Hey, girl. You wanna play?"

Unsure what the man wanted, Halo twitched her eyes to Cat. "Go on, Halo," Cat encouraged. "Take a toy!"

Halo sniffed each one and chose the animal. When she bit down in the middle, the toy made a satisfying *eek*. She chewed on it, loving the sound and the feel of the cloth-covered squeaker's resistance in her mouth.

Then something unexpected happened. The man took hold of one loop and gave a little yank. Taken off guard, Halo lost her grip for a second. She recovered in time to snatch the other loop in her teeth. They tussled over the toy for nearly a minute before the man let go.

Triumphant, Halo tossed her head to position the squeaker squarely between her jaws again. Giving it a good *eek-eek-eek* teething, she lay down, one paw firmly over the toy and one eye warily watching the man. No chance she was going to let him take it again.

Laughing, the man got to his feet. "Seems she's claimed her favorite."

Cat smiled. "Yeah. She likes the squeaker ones. Right, Halo?"

Halo lifted her head at the sound of her name. When Cat beckoned her, she snatched up the toy and sprang to her feet. Still on her lead, she trotted after Cat to an open area of grass, squeaking the toy the whole way and curious to see what other fun was in store.

That turned out to be training. Halo liked training with Cat, especially when Cat lavished her with kisses, hugs, and praise. When Cat took the tug toy and tucked it in her back pocket, though? She didn't like that quite as much. She'd chosen that toy. Had fought for the right to keep it. She wanted it back and didn't understand what she had to do to get it. But then Cat began a game of sit-and-stay. Halo had played it at home before, so she recognized the commands and realized that if she did as Cat instructed, she'd get to play with the toy again. Obeying the commands here, though—that was tough. She'd plant her rump on the ground just like she was supposed to. But when Cat started backing away, one hand on the lead and the other raised to signal Halo was to stay put, her haunches would rise up as if they had a mind of their own. There was just so much going on around her that she wanted to investigate!

Finally, she settled down enough to do what Cat wanted her to do. And when she did—oh, boy! Cat gave her the tug toy and wrestled and played with her! After that, her focus stayed squarely on Cat. They played three more rounds of sit-and-stay, and each one ended with her getting the toy as well as warm "Good girl, Halo!" praise and enthusiastic petting. Halo loved the rewards and attention and was eager to keep going. Instead, Cat led her back to her kennel, where a bowl of cool water waited for her. And that was good, too, she decided as she lapped up her drink.

Sweat trickled down Cat's back. It was late afternoon, and the Florida sunshine was still beating down with a vengeance. That's why she'd always chosen a breed with lighter-colored fur, like yellow Labs. Miami's sun was just too punishing on an all-black dog. Cat herself would have given anything to be wearing shorts, a T-shirt, and flip-flops. But at the FL-TF1 simulated disaster zone, you had to wear clothing that provided protection from rough, jagged surfaces. Long pants, long sleeves, and steel-toed boots made up everyone's standard outfit, and sometimes a safety helmet and thick leather gloves, too.

She studied Halo stretched out in her kennel, panting. The pup was holding up well despite the heat. Cat could have continued with her obedience training for a while longer. But that would have been a mistake. Halo might have become bored regardless of the tug toy playtime and praise. Boredom and training did not mix. Better to quit with the dog wanting more.

Cat took a long swig from her water bottle, then checked out the other dogs and handlers. Obedience, agility, rescue—each pair was working on some aspect of search and rescue. Some, like Halo, were beginners just learning the basic obedience commands. Others, like the sure-footed golden retriever crossing a high plank suspended between two uprights, had advanced to more complicated maneuvers after months of hard work.

Then there was the yellow Lab zigzagging through the rubble pile. That dog was getting close to testing for her FEMA US&R certification. Right now, she was hot on the trail of a "victim," a handler who had volunteered to hide in one of three identical bark barrels—giant plastic tubes lying on their sides and sealed at both ends so the dog couldn't see inside. As Cat watched, the Lab halted in front of one barrel, shoved its nose into a small cutout in the wooden cover, and began barking.

A ghost of a smile crossed Cat's lips. Fancy, Bella, Siren—they'd all sounded just like that dog. Not the bark so much, but the confidence in it. *The victim is here*, that bark announced. *I'm sure of it.*

Sure enough, thirty seconds later, the "victim" popped out. The dog's human partner raced up, showering the dog with praise and rewarding her with her special toy. The Lab wriggled with such extreme happiness that Cat laughed out loud.

Next to her, Halo let out a low whine. "Had enough rest?" Cat asked. "Okay, girl. Let's finish our day with something new."

With Halo on a lead at her side, she approached a young woman, a recent addition to Cat's group of handler trainees. "I'd like to try a little game of runaway with Halo. Want to be my victim?"

The woman laughed. "Can't say no to that!"

One goal of canine search and rescue training was to get the dog committed to locating a victim. But no dog started off knowing how to do that. It was up to their handlers to teach them. Runaway was one method they used.

Runaway involved three players—the handler, the dog, and the volunteer victim. While the handler controlled the dog on its lead, the victim got the dog interested in a toy. When the dog was fully engaged, the victim took control of the toy and ran away with it. Then the handler released the dog, who would go in search of the toy—and, in doing so, would locate the victim.

Cat handed the woman the animal squeaky toy Halo had played with earlier. "She's just starting out, so hide where she can see you."

"Got it." The woman stood in front of Halo and shook the toy. "You want this? Huh, Halo?" She infused her voice with enthusiasm and energy. "Here you go, Halo! Come and get it!"

Halo reacted right away, barking and jumping and lunging. For a puppy, she was so strong Cat had to work to keep her under control. But even as Cat's arm muscles struggled against the straining pup, her heart soared. Halo's impatience to follow the volunteer and get the toy was exactly what she wanted to see. That eagerness to give chase during training would one day translate to eagerness to search for a victim during a rescue mission.

At Cat's direction, the woman turned and fled, but only a short distance away to a wall made of concrete blocks. She stood in view, waving the toy where Halo could see it.

By now, Halo was in a frenzy of excitement. Cat retained her firm hold on the lead, and together, they raced to the victim's location. The woman immediately rewarded Halo with the toy while Cat heaped on praise.

"Good girl, Halo! Good girl!" she cried, rubbing her puppy's chin.

Eek-eek-eek, Halo responded through the squeaker, which made everyone in earshot crack up.

Halo had done well for her first time playing runaway. In the weeks and months ahead, the exercise would become increasingly complicated, with the victim partially visible, then totally hidden, and the distances farther, with obstacles and distractions scattered along the way.

But those challenges were a long time away. And while Cat believed Halo had what it took to master them, there was no guarantee. In the end, how Halo performed was up to Halo herself.

IT'S UP TO THE PUP

There's an old saying: you can lead a horse to water, but you can't make it drink. Meaning, you can't really control what someone else may or may not do. It's true for humans, and it's *definitely* true for canine search and rescue candidates.

"Owners think their dog will be great," Cat says. "And maybe they are great. Well trained, smart, fearless. But if a dog doesn't want to climb a rubble pile, or gives up before finding a victim, or decides squirrels are more interesting than search and rescue? Forget it. There isn't a whole lot you can do to change that dog's behavior. And honestly, you shouldn't try, not unless you want a stressed-out dog."

It isn't a question of the dog's obedience or ability. It's about the dog's mind-set and interest in the work. For some dogs, scouring through rubble and locating victims is the greatest job in the world. They'd do it all day long if they could. For others, though, it's a chore they want to avoid. Or worse, the training makes the dog anxious or even downright scared.

While it's important to give the dog a chance to recover and reconsider whether to continue, it's equally important to recognize when the dog has reached the end of the line with its training. And not just for the dog's sake.

"Imagine you're deployed on a mission," Cat says. "Lives depend on your dog doing this job. If your dog freezes or freaks out? Then those lives will be lost."

Bottom line? When it comes to pursuing a canine career in search and rescue, ultimately, it's up to the pup.

"Climb, Halo. Up! Up!"

Halo shifted from paw to paw and let out a keening whine of anxiety. She'd been coming to the US&R canine agility training grounds for several months now, so she understood what Cat wanted her to do. And if she'd been faced with any other obstacle, she probably would have given it a try. But she couldn't bring herself to do this one. The ladder was just too scary, with its near-vertical incline and the narrow, rounded rungs with yawing spaces in between. As surefooted as she was, those spaces spelled trouble. So, while she wanted to please Cat, she refused to obey.

After a long tense moment, she sensed Cat relax. "Okay, girl. We'll try again later."

Relieved, Halo spun in a happy circle, then followed Cat to the next challenge.

The agility grounds were set up like a doggy playground, with wooden climbing structures, a teeter-totter, a crawl-under bench, barrels of different heights, and more. But this playground wasn't for playtime. Here in this safe, controlled environment, Halo was learning to navigate over, under, through, and around the kinds of surfaces and obstacles she would likely encounter during a real-life rescue.

She gave an excited bark when they stopped at a two-level structure of inclined walkways, platforms, and narrow plank bridges. This was more like it—she'd been on this piece of equipment many times before. On her lead and with Cat keeping pace by her side, Halo hopped from the ground to a low barrel and then scampered up a walkway to a platform that came up to Cat's waist. She was about to step onto a bridge that connected to another platform when Cat's firm voice stopped her.

"Wait. Wait."

Halo huffed with impatience but obeyed. She sat and waited until finally, Cat gave the command to go, pairing it with a hand gesture indicating the direction. Halo trotted quickly across the bridge to the next platform where she waited again. Then, following Cat's next order, she jumped down to the grass and hurried with her to a different set of platforms by the back wall.

This was one of the trickier obstacles. A large square of wood, suspended at the corners by four chains, was set between two stationary stands. When Halo stepped onto the square, it shifted and swung underfoot. She might have tumbled off if Cat hadn't steadied her.

"That's a girl, Halo. Good girl." Her handler's calming voice, and the speed with which she'd helped her, tapped into Halo's trust in her—a bond that solidified more every time they worked together. With Cat by her side, Halo moved confidently from the wobbly platform and down to the grass.

Someone else was waiting for them there: Cat's friend Frank, another US&R dog trainer who worked in tandem with Cat. Halo had adored Frank since that first day when he'd played tug with her. She adored the tubular foam-and-cloth tug toy he held out to her even more. With a happy growl, she snatched the toy in her powerful jaws and whipped her head from side to side to free it from Frank's grasp.

"Man, she's even stronger than the last time we played!" Frank said with a gasping laugh.

Somehow, Frank got control. Halo froze, expecting him to drop the toy for a round of "Who can grab it first?" Instead, he hurried off, toy in hand. She lunged to follow, but Cat held her back on a tight lead. Halo gave a frantic bark as Frank disappeared inside one end of a dark L-shaped corrugated plastic tunnel. *Hey!* that bark meant. *I want that toy!*

As if she understood, Cat released her. Like a torpedo, Halo streaked across the grass and dove into the tunnel. It was hot and pitch-black inside, but she didn't slow until she came to the corner. She angled abruptly into the other half of the tunnel. Now she could see light at the far end—light, and Frank! She raced to him, and together, they tumbled out onto the grass. They tussled again. But this time, she ended up with the toy.

Two weeks later, Cat, Halo, and Frank met up at the agility park again. Her pup—no, her *dog*; though not quite a year old, Halo was almost full-grown and had energy to spare. Cat had been pleased with her progress in the agility park. The only disappointment was Halo's refusal to try the ladder. Cat had tried her a few more times since that first attempt but with the same result. It was frustrating, but even so—

"I want to try the ladder again," Cat told Frank.

Frank glanced up from playing tug-of-war with Halo. "You sure? Could be risky."

Cat knew what he meant. Trainers walked a fine line with their canines. Push too hard, and a dog that wasn't ready might start looking at that obstacle as a punishment rather than a challenge. Go too easy, though, and the dog might stop trying. Maybe Halo still wasn't ready for the ladder. But there was only one way to be sure. "Yeah. Let's give it a try." To Halo, she said, "Drop it."

Halo gave the toy a few more yanks before reluctantly letting go. Frank quickly stuffed it out of sight in his back pocket while Cat led Halo over to the ladder.

"Okay, girl." She patted and stroked her dog, then straightened. "Climb. Up! Up!"

Halo twitched her eyes from the ladder to Cat. She licked her chops, whined, and sidestepped away. Cat nudged her back with gentle insistence. "Come on, girl. You can do this. Climb!"

Halo whined again, and for a split second, Cat feared she'd refuse yet again. Then suddenly, Halo reared up and hooked her front paws on the third rung. Her back feet did a quick two-step on the ground, as if she wanted to lift them up but was unsure where to put them.

This was a tipping point. Cat could allow Halo to drop back to the ground and then try again another day. Or she could begin teaching her how to maneuver the rungs. She chose to teach, scooping Halo up under her rear and carefully placing her back paws on the bottom rung before releasing her. "Climb, Halo!" she encouraged.

Halo tried. But like all dogs first learning the ladder, she pushed off with both back feet, bunny-hop style. Dogs naturally leaped that way, not by moving one foot then the other, so Cat had been expecting it. And a good thing, too, for one of Halo's back paws slipped sideways. The other flailed about in thin air.

"It's okay, girl, I gotcha!" Cat caught Halo in her strong arms to keep her from falling. She supported Halo and, murmuring words of praise, helped her grope with her front paws up the remaining rungs and onto the platform. She immediately whipped the toy from her pocket and gave it to her panting dog.

"Oh, good girl, Halo," Cat cried. "Such a good girl!" As she mouthed and squeaked the toy, Halo's tail wagged so hard her whole backside wriggled.

Cat knew Halo had attempted the ladder for the squeaker toy and for the praise. She'd kept going when she faltered because she trusted Cat would catch her. But there was a greater reason she climbed: because she wanted to. Trainers could use any number of teaching techniques and methods of encouragement to coax their dogs to do something. At the end of the day, though, it came down to the dog's desire to work and learn. You couldn't teach that. Either the dog had that drive, or it didn't.

Halo had proven to Cat yet again that she had it. And that was good, because what lay ahead was infinitely more challenging than climbing a five-rung ladder.

A REAL-LIFE RESCUE

Hot dust coated Cat's clothes and clung to her face and hair. A stench more horrible than any she'd ever smelled before threatened to make her gag. But the devastation sprawled out before her...the acres and acres of rubble and ruin...that was worst of all.

It was January 14, 2010. Two days earlier, the island nation of Haiti had been rocked by a catastrophic earthquake and powerful aftershocks. Buildings collapsed, killing thousands and trapping hundreds more. Without immediate help, those trapped would die, too.

Relief teams from around the world were activated within hours of the quake, including Cat's team, Florida Task Force 1 (FL-TF1). As she boarded the transport plane with her yellow Lab, Bella, she had tried to imagine the chaos that lay ahead. Now, as she gazed at Haiti's capital, Port-au-Prince, she saw the reality was much worse than anything her mind had conjured up.

Beside her, Bella gave a low whine. Cat caught one of her dog's silky ears between her fingers. She rubbed it for a moment, then let go and straightened. "Okay, enough standing around," she said to no one in particular. "We're here to help save lives. So let's get going."

For the next few days, Cat and Bella and five other FL-TF1 canine-and-human pairs took turns combing the capital city's rubble for survivors. They weren't alone. Hundreds of first responders, aid workers, engineers, and construction crews descended on Port-au-Prince and the surrounding areas to hand out supplies, administer emergency medical treatment, shore up buildings close to collapse, and clear streets to make way for trucks and rescue vehicles. Conditions were horrible—no running water or sanitary facilities, little food, limited electrical services, and hazardous surroundings, all cloaked in oppressive heat, choking dust, and the heartbreaking gloom of death.

Yet within the bleakness were pockets of pure joy—moments triggered by a dog suddenly letting out its special bark to alert its human partner of a survivor. The rescues that followed those barks were always dangerous, both for the victims trapped within the shifting rubble and the crew working with painstaking care to free them. But seeing those survivors pulled to safety, hearing about other teams' rescues, and witnessing loved ones reunited after days of anguished uncertainty...that was what kept Cat and the others pushing forward.

Even so, as the days ticked by, Cat's morale began to flag. Before it sunk too low, though, there came a story that lifted her spirits and those of everyone who heard it.

Working on a tip, Cat's friend and fellow FL-TF1 handler Steve Driscoll was checking out a nearby village. The mountainside houses had been reduced to trash heaps of metal and wood and concrete by the earthquake. The possibility of locating even one survivor in those ruins so many days after the quake seemed remote. But one villager insisted she could hear her child crying there. If there was even a chance she was right...

Steve sent his border collie, Blaze, to investigate. Blaze disappeared from view in the destruction. Long moments passed. Then—

Woof! Woof! Woof!

Steve and other rescuers picked their way to Blaze's location next to a solid wall of concrete. Could there really be a child trapped behind it? Steve trusted his dog. So they drilled a hole in the slab and then shined a flashlight into the opening. Sure enough, staring at them from the other side was a small girl. A girl who might not have survived if not for Blaze.

In all, Cat's Florida team saved eleven people in Haiti. "Those are moms, dads, and children who get to grow up and become something and have families of their own," Cat reflected. "Without our dogs, I don't think those people would have been found."

While Bella didn't alert on anyone, she was still a valuable part of the canine team, for when she reported for duty at Cat's side, another dog could rest before its next shift. And a rested dog was a dog ready to do its job—the job of helping save lives.

"Here go you, Halo! Kick it to me!"

Rump in the air and tail beating back and forth, Halo clasped the small soccer ball between her front paws and eyed Cat's boy, Lance. He eyed her back from his spot at the other end of the yard, his arms wide and his feet planted in the grass. "Come on, girl!" he called. "Kick it!"

Halo didn't need more encouragement. She darted forward, batting the ball ahead of her with her paws, snatching it up between her teeth, and then dropping it to kick it a few more times until it reached Lance's feet. Laughing, he scooped it up.

"Ready?"

Halo bounced and spun with an excited bark. *Go*

on! Do it! Do it! When Lance booted the ball on a soaring arc to the other end of the yard, she streaked after it, her strong paws tearing up tufts of grass as she sprinted. She overran the ball, skidded to a stop, and raced back to begin all over again.

Halo loved playing soccer—loved balls in general, actually, ever since Cat's mother had given Halo her first one back when she was a puppy. She never missed a chance to chase them, gnaw on them, carry them around in her mouth, and kick them through the grass. She found them in all kinds of places, except one: the US&R training site. She'd never seen a single ball there. Until now.

The sun was beating down as usual on the training site that morning. Halo's tongue lolled out the side of her mouth, dripping the occasional drop of drool onto the hot sand-and-dirt ground. Beside her, Cat smelled of sweat mingled with deodorant and the well-loved chew toy stashed in her pocket.

The shade-free course in front of Halo promised to be just as sweltering. The area was laid out like a baseball diamond. At the corners where first, second, and third base would be, there were platforms, each set at a different height. A fourth platform stood in the middle where the pitcher's mound and rubber would be located. Halo and Cat stood at home base, waiting for a golden retriever named Rocky to finish his turn.

But Rocky was more interested in lounging and panting than following his handler's instructions. After a few final attempts to get his dog to obey, the handler gave up. With Rocky's lead in hand, he approached the dog, who immediately rolled over onto his back and presented his belly for a rub. The handler gave a little chuckle and obliged.

"No, no, no," Cat muttered as the man snapped on the lead, gave Rocky's belly one last pet, and then led the golden retriever off to the side.

Halo glanced up, her brow puckered and ears forward. But Cat wasn't chastising her. Her eyes were on Rocky and his handler. Cat gave a quick shake of her head, then leaned down and removed Halo's lead.

"Okay, girl. Ready?"

Halo stood up and wagged her tail.

"Good girl. Go out!" Cat flung her arm forward, pointing straight ahead.

Halo headed to the pitcher's mound. At Cat's next command—"Hup!"—she jumped onto the platform.

"Sit!" Cat called. Halo turned in a quick circle and sat, eyes and ears on her handler. "Wait!" Halo panted atop the structure until Cat pointed in a different direction, toward third base. "Over, Halo. Over!"

Halo jumped off the first platform and started toward the next. But midway across, something in the infield between second and third caught her eye. Something small and round.

A ball? *Here?*

Halo immediately veered off course to investigate. Focused intently on her target, she was only dimly aware that Cat was calling to her. She reached the object and was disappointed to discover it wasn't a ball at all, just a smooth gray rock half-buried in the dirt. Heavy and cumbersome in the mouth, rocks were nowhere near as much fun as balls.

Then again, they often had a nice, salty taste. She dug at it with her front paws, then sampled it with a few licks.

Hm. More dust than salt. Still...she started digging again.

"Halo! Leave it!"

Cat's sharp voice finally penetrated Halo's brain. She paused and looked over at her handler. Hands on hips. Lips tight. Eyes narrowed and piercing beneath the brim of her baseball cap. Cat's body language spoke even more plainly than her voice. Halo got the message loud and clear: *I'm not pleased.*

Then Cat relaxed. "Over, Halo." She gestured toward third base. "Over."

Halo snuffled the rock one more time before abandoning it to lope to the indicated platform.

Cat yanked off her baseball cap, ran her fingers through her sweat-soaked hair, and put the cap back on. *That dog is* so *testing my patience today*, she thought as she tugged her ponytail through the cap's back opening.

Halo had returned to investigate the rock two more times during her direction and control training session. Each time, Cat had managed to get her back on course by only using visual and audible commands. But regaining Halo's attention hadn't been easy. And that had Cat worried.

To become a certified FEMA US&R canine, Halo would undergo a five-part test: Obedience, Bark Indication, Direction and Control, Agility, and Rubble

Pile. Fail even one of those parts, and she would not earn her certification. Unfortunately, her performance during today's trial run of direction and control had not been good. If she acted like that during the real test...she would fail the whole thing.

I know she's smart enough to do it, Cat thought as she fastened the lead to Halo's collar. *Question is, can she stay on task, or will she get distracted when it counts?*

More training would help, she knew. Not today, though. Halo was a driven dog, eager and willing to work. But she might burn out if she was put through the same exercises too many times. Plus, the heat was making the day extra hard for both of them. Cat looked forward to getting home and jumping into her new in-ground pool. Unfortunately, there was one last thing she had to do before she left—and it was something she never enjoyed.

She stowed Halo in a kennel and went in search of the man who'd been on the course before them. She found him with Rocky in the parking area, chatting with two other FL-TF1 recruits. She caught his eye and waved him over. Rocky flopped on the ground between them.

"Hey, Brad," Cat said. "Listen. You and Rocky have been coming here for a couple of months now, right?"

"Yeah, and it's been great," Brad said enthusiastically. "I mean, I know Rocky isn't really into training on hot days like this, but I think he's starting to get the hang of some of this stuff, don't you?"

Cat wanted to agree. Like her, Brad was a first responder. He already knew what it was like to jump feetfirst into an emergency, which made him a great candidate for US&R. But his dog had been eight months old when they began training, and now he was nearly a year old. The ideal starting age for canine trainees was closer to three months. She had a name for good-natured, well-loved but untrained dogs Rocky's age: pets.

"Actually," she told Brad bluntly, "I'm not so sure Rocky is catching on. Or that he ever will."

Brad looked surprised. "Come again?"

"Dogs here fall into two categories," Cat explained. "Those who are driven and those who aren't." She crouched down next to Rocky, who gave her a wide toothy grin as she ruffled his ears. "Rocky is a total love, but he's not driven."

"That's something we can work on, though, right?"

Brad persisted. "Find a way to motivate him? I mean, at least he's not crazy like some other dogs here."

Cat stood up. "In my experience, you can work with a crazy dog, channel and tame its energy, and turn it into a good search and rescue dog. But you can never truly motivate an unmotivated dog."

She didn't add that giving Rocky belly rubs when he disobeyed commands, as she'd seen Brad do earlier, only reinforced the dog's unwanted behavior. Instead, she outlined some exercises he could try with Rocky at home. "Who knows?" she said. "Maybe he'll be the exception that proves the rule. If so, come on back in a few months and we'll take another look at him."

But as Brad and Rocky drove off, she knew she'd seen the last of the beautiful golden retriever. She'd had to dismiss other canines before, for being too aggressive or too timid, for failing to learn basic commands, for being too easily distracted. It was never any fun. But the type of work these dogs were being trained for was too important to waste valuable time on candidates who would never make it.

She could only hope Halo would continue to excel. If not... well, she'd have to dismiss her own dog.

COULD YOU HANDLE BEING A HANDLER?

Being part of FEMA's elite canine task force is hard work. The dogs go through months of rigorous training and face tough challenges on search and rescue missions. But they aren't in it alone. Their handlers—or human partners—are with them every step of the way, guiding them, learning with them, and working alongside them.

So, what does it take to make it as a handler?

Commitment, for one thing. Becoming a search and rescue dog handler is a months-long process and 100 percent volunteer. It starts with a four-day course during which recruits learn the basics of dog training and how to select a puppy, and they agree to uphold a high standard of moral and ethical behavior.

When the course is done and they've adopted a puppy, the hands-on training begins. Here, physical fitness and stamina play a huge role. For two-plus years, human partners will navigate acres of rubble, climb up massive debris piles, crawl through tunnels and under overhangs, and run agility courses alongside their dog. They'll play victim and hide in cramped spaces so searching dogs can find them. Obedience sessions, socialization outings, and aggression control—these all require handlers to have a certain level of fitness to be successful.

Endurance and fitness are even more important at an actual disaster site. There, handlers work long hours for days, or sometimes weeks, in horrendous, dangerous conditions. Fires and floods; earthquake aftershocks and shifting buildings; torrential rain, whiteout snow, baking heat, gale force winds—anything is possible. And when a dog locates a survivor, the handler will most likely have to navigate unstable, even treacherous, terrain to reach the spot and confirm the find.

These same crisis conditions require a handler to be mentally tough. "You'll see blood and trauma and injured, crying kids and innocent animals who are suffering. *Everyone* is suffering," Cat says. "You have to push through your feelings and use your training and do your job. And when you do that," she adds, "you can sleep at night knowing you and your dog did everything you possibly could to help."

Being a search and rescue dog handler isn't for everyone. But for those who rise to the challenges, it's life-changing. "It's a passion," Cat explains. "I love what I do."

"Speak," Frank commanded.

Rowf! Rowf! Rowf! Eyes on the tug toy in Frank's hand, Halo let out three loud barks.

"Good girl!" Frank shook the toy in front of her. She lunged and grabbed the free end in her teeth. Cat joined them as Frank and Halo wrestled and tugged. "Good girl, Halo!"

Halo was playing runaway, one of her favorite games, with Frank and Cat. This round had been a little confusing, though. In the past, she could always see at least part of Frank. This time, he'd disappeared completely behind a pile of pallets. She'd hesitated when Cat ordered her to search. It was only after she heard Frank's voice calling her name that she'd pinpointed his location.

The command to speak was new, too, but not confusing. She liked barking—did it a lot, in fact—and barking after finding Frank made total sense to her. How else would she show her excitement at discovering her friend?

"Drop it, Halo," Cat ordered. She snapped Halo's lead to her collar. "Drop it."

Halo dropped the toy. Frank snatched it up and put it behind his back. Halo darted toward him, straining against the lead, eager to get hold of the toy again. When Frank ran off with the toy and vanished from view once again, that eagerness rose to a whole new level. She lunged and pulled and let out a string of frantic barks. She wanted to see Frank. To go after him. And most of all, she wanted to get her toy.

"Wait," Cat warned.

Halo stopped lunging, but her whole body quivered with anticipation. With one hand firmly clutching her collar, Cat moved behind her and laid her other hand lightly on her torso. Halo registered the touch but didn't take her eyes off the place where Frank had disappeared.

There was a click as Cat took off the lead. "Ready? Search!"

Zoom! Her lean, muscular legs working in perfect rhythm, Halo streaked across the ground like a rocket. This time, she found Frank faster.

"Speak!"

Again, Halo barked, and then, finally, wonderfully, she received her reward of tussle time with her toy.

They played more rounds of this new version of runaway. Frank never hid in the same place twice. Once, he was behind the nearby rock pile. It was a piece of kibble finding him there—she could hear the rocks shifting under his body. The next time was a little harder because she had to run a great distance to get to his hiding spot by a huge concrete storm tube. Luckily, she caught a whiff of him in the air when she was near his location. Otherwise, she would have run right past him. Each time she located him, he commanded her to speak.

Slowly, a little seed of understanding took root in Halo's mind: *Good things happen when I bark after finding Frank. So, from now on, I'm going to bark when I find him.*

"She's doing well with her bark alert and now-you-see-me, now-you-don't runaway," Cat commented to Frank three months later. "I want to see what she does with a blind search."

"You sure she's ready?" Frank replied doubtfully. "Could be trouble if you push her too soon."

Cat toed a piece of gravel out of the dirt. She trusted Frank's opinion more than any other dog handler's. Still, after working with Halo every week for the past year and a half, she thought her dog was ready for the next crucial phase.

That phase was training Halo to air scent. Bloodhounds and other breeds with hypersensitive noses automatically defaulted to their sense of smell when tracking humans. One sniff of the victim's clothing was all they needed to follow the scent along the ground. Halo's sense of smell was nothing compared to that of a bloodhound. So instead of using her nose, she relied on her vision and her hearing to zero in on her targets.

The trouble with that was that victims in urban

disasters were usually out of sight—buried beneath rubble, trapped in a collapsed building, imprisoned inside a wreck. Most times, they were also unconscious. Out cold, they were unable to shout or make other noises to attract attention. There was something all humans did, though, no matter where they were or what condition they were in: they always gave off a scent.

An Urban Search and Rescue dog detects and tracks a victim by first discovering the victim's scent cone—a plume of odor that radiates out from the victim, with the victim at the cone's point. There, the scent is super saturated and concentrated. Move away from the victim, and the scent becomes fainter and more diffused as it spreads over an ever-widening area. Search and rescue dogs are trained to recognize they are in a scent cone and to sniff through the air to the cone's point—and the victim's location.

If Halo was to become one of those dogs, she needed to learn to use her nose. It was the hardest thing to teach, and the most vital thing to learn. Blind finds, where the dog doesn't see the victim hide or have any visual or auditory clues to the victim's whereabouts, were the first lesson in training her to air scent.

"Well," Cat said finally, "she's gotta start sometime. Might as well be today."

"Right." Frank jerked his chin toward a concrete wall. "The wind is coming from that direction, so I'll hide over there. Give her a fighting chance to scent me."

Cat nodded. To give the dog the best chance of a successful find, all air scent training started with the victim being upwind of the dog. That way, the smell was carried to the dog's nose on the wind.

Frank got Halo all riled up with her tug toy, then took control of the toy. Cat distracted Halo while Frank ran off to tuck himself behind the wall. Once Frank was completely hidden, Cat positioned Halo so she was facing the right direction and said, "Ready? Ready? Search!"

Tail whipping excitedly, Halo bounded up, trotted forward a few steps, faltered, and stopped. The backward glance she gave Cat was so comically confused Cat had to bite her lip to keep from laughing. "Search!" she repeated.

Halo twisted her head this way and that. Her ears swiveled. She headed one way and then another. Suddenly, something caught her attention, and like a flash, she was off.

Unfortunately, the something was a feral cat, one of many that made their home at the FL-TF1 training facility. It took Cat several minutes to get Halo to return. She reattached the lead and called to Frank to come out.

"So. *That* happened," she said wryly.

Frank clapped her shoulder. "Early days yet. She'll get there."

Cat hoped he was right. Because if Halo couldn't master the blind search and air scent, then everything they'd accomplished in the past year and a half would have been for nothing.

A GLIMPSE INSIDE DISASTER CITY

A leg pokes out the window of a train wreck. A woman hunkers down next to a collapsed movie theater. At a nearby strip mall, a man lies pinned beneath a heap of brick and metal and glass.

Don't worry. These people are just volunteers pretending to be real victims at Disaster City, the site in Texas where Halo trained. Disaster City is part of the Texas A&M Engineering Extension, or TEEX, the country's largest complex of simulated disasters. Built to mirror the aftermath of real-life catastrophes, the fifty-two-acre TEEX facility is prime training grounds for multiple first responders. Canine handlers and their dogs, among others, come from all over the world to learn new techniques and practice their emergency skills amid the all-too-realistic wreckage. Without this hands-on experience, they might not be prepared to handle wide-scale disasters that, sadly, require them to be ready for action at a moment's notice.

"I've been to TEEX a bunch of times," Cat says.

"The place has everything, and not just for dogs. There's a huge outdoor area dedicated to firefighting techniques, another for dealing with hazardous materials. There's training for people who want to learn emergency operations management—you know, the folks who coordinate the search and rescue missions. Basically, if it has anything to do with emergency response, it's probably at TEEX."

Still, the canine training at Disaster City is what brings Cat back to TEEX year after year. "Sometimes I go there with my own dogs, sometimes with new handlers as their instructor. Each experience there has been amazing."

Like the time she and Halo took part in a simulated urban disaster rescue. Strapped together with harnesses, they leaped off a rooftop and zipped down a long line over smoking rubble to the debris-ridden ground. And another time when, instead of finding a volunteer hidden beneath old blankets and cushions in the train wreck, Halo snuffled a half-eaten hamburger planted as a distraction. "Yeah, I didn't know whether to laugh or groan when she did that," Cat recalls. "Luckily, she moved on and found the victim eventually!"

One other bonus to training dogs at TEEX? The relationships forged before, during, and after the simulated disasters. "Thanks to Disaster City and other facilities like it," Cat says, "I've gotten to know people who serve on other FEMA Task Forces. These are people who might be deployed to the same disaster as FL-TF1. Knowing how well we work together during simulated catastrophes gives me confidence in how we'll perform when the real thing hits."

Halo flew over the ground. The long line attached to her collar trailed behind her. The other end was in Cat's hand. Her destination was a row of identical ridged plastic barrels lying on their sides. Wooden lids sealed the front openings, a single small mousehole carved out of the bottom of each. There were eight barrels in all, but only one contained the prize: Frank.

Halo reached the first barrel and stuck her nose in the mousehole. After a moment's snuffling, she moved on. Nothing of interest in there unless you considered musty plastic smells interesting, which she didn't. The second barrel held the same odor, as did the third. But the fourth barrel—*Yes! Result!*

Halo started barking. She flicked a look at Cat, who stood with a few other handlers. Cat looked back but made no move to come investigate her find. Halo barked louder, more insistently. Still Cat hung back. Finally, after a long stretch of on-again, off-again barks, Cat trotted forward and pulled off the wooden cover. Halo darted into the barrel excitedly, dug at the contents inside, then hurried back out again.

Toy time! Toy time! With happy little woofs, she bounced on her front paws expectantly.

Cat squatted down and reached into the barrel. "Sorry, Halo." She pulled out the contents. "It's just a pile of old clothes, girl. Not Frank. Just clothes." She replaced the clothes, repositioned the lid, and stood up.

Halo stopped bouncing. *No toy? Why no toy?* Her mind whirred as she put it together. *I barked when I found stinky old clothes. Barking at stinky old clothes did not get me a toy. So, I shouldn't bark when I find stinky old clothes.*

Then something else clicked. *Wait! Where's Frank?*

"Halo, search!" Cat ordered, backing away to her spot.

Halo took a step toward the first barrel, then corrected herself—*nothing there, not even clothes*—and stuck her nose in the mousehole of barrel number five. It was a dud. She raced to the next.

Yes-yes-yes-yes-yes! Even before her snout reached number six's cutout, the scent wafting from the hole hit her nostril receptors and painted an image of Frank in her mind's eye. She snuffled the hole just to be sure, then sat and let out a series of loud, confident barks.

After what seemed like forever, the wooden cover trembled, then fell forward at her feet. Frank crawled out, shaking Halo's favorite tug toy. "You found me! Good girl! Good girl!"

The other handlers cheered and applauded, too. Cat hurried up, laughing and smiling. "Yes, Halo! Yes! That's my girl! That's my good, good girl!"

Halo wriggled and danced and gnawed the tug toy. *Find Frank. Bark. Get toy. I understand this game*, her happy dance proclaimed. *And I like it.*

"Why do you always put Frank or one of us in the barrel?" asked the young woman walking alongside

Cat. "Why not someone Halo isn't familiar with? I mean, she won't be searching for someone she knows at a real disaster site."

"I hope not," Cat said dryly. She adjusted her hold on Halo's lead. She and the woman, a recent handler trainee, were taking Halo for a loop around the block while Frank reset the barrels for another search. He'd change their position in the lineup, moving the barrel of old clothes and the one with the food stash, which Halo hadn't alerted on this round, to different spots. He'd move his barrel, too, but make sure to hide in the same one so it would stay "hot," or saturated with his scent. Spreading his smell from barrel to barrel was a bad idea; it would only confuse and frustrate Halo.

Not frustrating Halo, Cat now explained to the trainee, was why she used Frank or another Task Force teammate in the barrels. "Asking Halo to find someone she's never met or smelled before at this stage in her training isn't fair. I want her to succeed. She knows what Frank smells like, so she's got a much better chance of locating him. Of being successful."

Halo had been doing well with barrel searches since first being introduced to the exercise months ago. Cat had started out with just three barrels, two empty and the hot one with Frank inside. After a few weeks, Halo had seemed to understand that finding Frank was the goal. Learning to bark alert for thirty seconds, though—that had come on more gradually. Even now, Cat could see Halo questioning how much longer she needed to stay put at her find.

Cat got that. Thirty seconds was a long time for her to wait, too. But rules were rules: to pass her upcoming Foundation Skills Assessment, or FSA, Halo had to stay at a find and bark at least three times within a thirty-second time period. In a real disaster, that sustained bark would alert Cat that Halo had located something—or hopefully, *someone*—and that rescuers needed to get to the spot pronto.

After several sessions of Halo correctly identifying the hot barrel, Cat had gradually upped the difficulty. From three barrels they went to five, four empty and one hot. Sometimes a different person than Frank, but always someone Halo was very familiar with, hid inside. When Cat was satisfied with Halo's competence at that level, she added other challenges. She stashed old clothes ripe with body odor in one barrel and in another, a stash of food that, while inaccessible to Halo, sent out an enticing smell. Changing the positions of the barrels, increasing the number of barrels, adding or taking away other odor-producing items—the training had many variations, and Cat tested Halo on them all.

It took time for Halo to get up to speed after each change. At first, she barked whenever she scented anything other than an empty barrel's stale air. Using positive reinforcement of toys and wildly enthusiastic praise, Cat trained her to bark alert only when she found Frank or another of their teammates. Throughout every step, she helped Halo be successful. Steering her in the right direction with the long line when she veered off course. Guiding her to the right barrel even, to strengthen the message that *this* was where she should end up. And she made sure to correct bad habits—circling the barrels before sniffing the mouseholes, for instance, or doing a little dance before barking—before they became established routines. In the midst of a real disaster, such routines would take up precious time that a victim clinging to life didn't have to spare.

Finding that victim—that's what Cat ultimately needed Halo to succeed at. Together, they'd made great strides toward that goal in the past months. In fact, Cat was feeling confident enough in Halo's progress that she planned to put Halo through mock trials of the two FEMA US&R canine certification tests: the FSA, where her obedience, agility, and search skills would be evaluated, and then the more challenging Certification Evaluation, or CE. Pass both official tests, and Halo would take her place at Cat's side in future urban disaster rescue missions as a fully certified member of Florida Task Force 1's canine unit.

And if Halo failed? Well, much as Cat didn't want to admit it, failure was always a possibility. Which was why she kept pushing Halo, moving her forward, training her with new and different and more challenging exercises like the advanced barrel search.

"Okay, Halo," she said as she and the trainee completed their loop. "Let's go again."

TESTING, TESTING!

To be certified as a FEMA US&R canine, a dog must pass two exams: the Foundation Skills Assessment, or FSA, and the Certification Evaluation, or CE.

The FSA tests the canine in five areas. Here are the guidelines:

Obedience: The canine demonstrates that it is well-behaved and non-aggressive around strangers and in crowds. It heels at its handler's side on the lead. Off lead, it comes to an immediate emergency stop upon command. It stays for five minutes when out of sight of its handler.

Bark Indication: The dog scents, follows, and then correctly identifies the location of a hidden victim by barking at the location at least three times and for a period of thirty seconds—all with minimal direction from the handler.

Direction and Control: Off lead and in a course that includes one elevated area, the dog follows audible and visual commands from its handler that direct it to go right, left, backward, and forward; to stop; to wait; and then go back to the handler's side.

Agility: The canine navigates through a series of obstacles that simulate rubble conditions—unstable and slippery surfaces, various elevations, tight and dark spaces—off lead and with its handler following along behind.

Rubble Site: The dog is released on a real rubble site pile where volunteer victims are hidden and the dog's command of the four previous elements is put to the ultimate test. The dog must find and bark alert on two victims within fifteen minutes.

The CE test is a two-part practical exam, with both parts taking place on rubble piles. If the canine passes both, it is certified to be deployable with its handler and the Task Force on the next search and rescue mission.

Limited Access: The test gets its name because the handler is limited in the direction that can be given

URBAN SEARCH & RESCUE CANINE CERTIFICATION EXAM

TEST #1

Mastering stop, stay, and heel.

Each dog must walk alongside their handler in a group of people while frequently changing directions.

TEST #2

Bark to alert your handler.

Each dog must bark for 30 seconds after picking up on a scent.

TEST #3

Navigate on voice & hand signals.

Each dog must navigate a course by following only voice and hand signals. At times, a dog and its handler are over 50 feet apart.

TEST #4

Show your agility.

Each dog must successfully navigate a course consisting of a ladder, an elevated plank, a wobbly surface, and a tunnel.

TEST #5

Complete a simulated search.

Dog and handler teams prove they're worthy of FEMA certification by completing missions on two simulated disaster scenes.

to the dog during a twenty-minute search period to find at least one victim in a rubble pile while out of sight of its handler. When the dog locates the victim, it barks no less than three times to signal its handler of the find. The handler then has a choice: mark the site as a victim or declare it to be a false indication. If it's a false indication, then the handler instructs the dog to continue searching.

Full Access: On a different rubble pile, the handler directs and controls the canine throughout the twenty-minute search period for victims. Again, the dog must bark alert three times in a row, and the handler must decide if it is a true find or a false indication. Up to six victims can be found within the time frame—but no false finds are allowed! If a dog convinces its handler that there is a victim where no victim exists, then that dog will fail the test.

If a dog doesn't pass its first attempt at certification, its handler can take it back for more training and then retake the tests in three to six months' time. But with no guarantee that the dog will succeed the second time around, the handler might come to a heart-wrenching conclusion: despite months of hard work and promising successes at the training grounds, the dog isn't suited for the role of a search and rescue canine after all.

"Heel!"

Off lead, Halo walked alongside Cat through a crowd of people wandering about the FL-TF1 training site. The people didn't stand in their way, but they didn't step aside, either. Instead, Halo and Cat wove their way in and among them. They turned right. Left. Then right again. Cat abruptly quickened her pace. Halo matched it, and then slowed when Cat slowed. Always by her side. Always attuned to her movements.

Finally, Cat signaled for her to turn about. "Stop," she commanded.

Halo halted. Moments passed. Then Cat reached down and secured her collar around her neck. "Good girl," she said. "Good girl!"

Halo wagged her tail. She was pleased that Cat was happy with her performance. Not that she'd done anything unusual; after two years of training, staying at Cat's side and obeying her commands was ingrained behavior. Almost instinctual.

She understood exactly what Cat expected her to do during the next set of exercises, too. When Cat instructed her to sit and wait, she sat and waited, even when minute after long minute ticked by and Cat was out of her sight. She bolted up and charged forward when Cat finally gave the order to come, then stopped mid-run when Cat commanded her to stop. During a test of her and another dog's self-control, she sat frozen in place by Cat's side when the other dog and its human partner walked around them. She didn't even react when the walking dog got into her personal space—well, other than to stop panting and tense up for a second, that is.

After each exercise, Cat showered her with praise. Halo returned it with adoring looks and excited tail wags.

Later, Cat led her to a row of three covered barrels. At her command, Halo sprinted to the first, sniffed the mousehole, moved on to the second and sniffed there, and then went to the third before returning to the second. No doubt in her mind: someone was inside there. She glanced at Cat, looking for a signal. Cat raised her hand.

Rowf! Rowf! Rowf! Halo pressed her nose to the mousehole again. *Rowf! Rowf! Rowf!* She dug at the hole with her front paws, trying to claw off the lid. *Rowf! Rowf! Rowf!* She danced from one side of the hole to the other. Bark, sniff, dig, dance, bark, sniff, dig, dance—until at last Cat hurried up. "Good job, Halo! Good girl!"

Halo barked and wagged her tail and grabbed the tug toy Cat held out. Head high and squeaker squeaking, she trotted alongside Cat off the field. Her ears pricked when she heard a light scraping sound, and she glanced over her shoulder in time to see the barrel lid pop off and a teenage boy crawl out. She gave a little huff of satisfaction then as if to say, "Yup. Told you someone was in there."

The fun continued with a visit to the baseball-diamond-shaped course, where Cat sent her to wait on one elevated platform after another. Then it was on to the agility area. There, she keyed into Cat's commands. Up an incline. Over a bridge to a platform.

"Wait." Pause. Pause. Pause. "Over." Across another bridge and onto a shaky platform. "Wait." More pausing. Then another command from Cat that sent her trotting down an inclined walkway and over to—

The ladder. Halo halted, but only for a second. Then she climbed, one-two, three-four, front feet and back feet moving individually, until she reached the top and edged out onto the last platform and down another incline. Last and best of all was the L-shaped tunnel. She shot in one end, cornered hard at the angle, and raced out the other.

Cat was waiting for her at the end of the tunnel. Her broad smile signaled one emotion: pride. Cat knelt, and Halo launched herself into her open, waiting arms and wriggled with pleasure while Cat pet and praised her.

As special as that celebration was, it was nothing compared to the joy they shared just a short while later. Halo had been set loose on the rubble pile. Following her nose and moving with nimble grace, she scouted about in search of the two hidden victims. She identified the locations of both, each squashed into different tiny pockets of space beneath the concrete mounds.

"You did it, girl!" Cat cried ecstatically when they reunited beside the pile. "Oh, such a good girl, Halo! You are amazing!"

Fancy. Bella. Siren. In less than twenty-four hours, Halo would follow in their pawsteps and take the Certification Evaluation.

Cat glanced down to where her dog lay curled up in a tight ball. Half her muscular brown-black body was under the airplane seat in front of her. The other was tucked neatly between Cat's feet. Her lead hung loosely in Cat's hand.

Not that I need it, she thought, rubbing the lead's rough surface with her thumb. Halo was beautifully behaved, just as she had been on their first flight together from Detroit more than two years ago, and on other flights since—to Tennessee, Texas, and New York, where they trained together at those states' US&R facilities. Halo was permitted to ride in the cabin with Cat because Cat was a member of FEMA. Passengers who narrowed their eyes at the sleek, powerful dog resting on the floor by her feet quickly changed their expressions to respect and appreciation when they saw Cat's uniform. And of course, Halo's exemplary behavior helped—*Better than many children and even some adults,* Cat thought.

Today, she and Halo were returning to New York. To Fresh Kills Landfill on Staten Island, to be exact, where the CE would be held. Halo had passed her Foundation Skills Assessment with flying colors, although Cat had a moment of panic when Halo hesitated at the bottom of the ladder. Now, there were two more hurdles to go through for Halo to be certified for deployment: the Limited Access and Full Access Rubble Piles.

Cat knew what to expect, and yet her stomach flip-flopped when she thought about the next day's tests. Things could go wrong so easily, even for a dog as well trained and driven as Halo. The New York site had the same mountainous piles of broken concrete and glass, twisted metal, and construction debris as their home site. But having the same kind of rubble didn't make the piles *familiar.* The strangeness added another wrinkle to the tests' difficulty, but she couldn't help that.

She also couldn't help the nerves wracking her system when she arrived at Fresh Kills the next morning. So much was riding on the next few hours.

Halo can always retest in three months if she fails. Cat pushed the thought away the second it popped into her head. While true, she refused to approach the CE with that attitude.

Instead, she took Halo's lead firmly in hand and led her over to where other dogs and their handlers were gathering. The US&R canine community was relatively small, so she recognized some people. Besides those who were testing for the first time, a few of the dog and human pairs were likely there for recertification, she guessed, something FEMA required every three years.

Also on site were the people involved with coordinating and administering the test: the incident commander, or IC, who oversaw the whole event; one chief, two lead, and four additional evaluators who judged the dogs' abilities and awarded pass-fail marks for their performances; and multiple support personnel, from safety and emergency medical officers to timers, volunteer victims, and more.

Cat was chatting with a friend when the IC called for attention. She went over the rules, including codes of conduct and dismissal for canine aggression. Then she cleared her throat and changed topics.

"Staten Island is just a stone's throw away from Manhattan," she said with a backward wave toward the New York City skyline, "where one of the worst urban disasters in our history occurred on September 11, 2001. Within hours, canine task forces from across the country were combing the World Trade Center rubble for victims. Sadly, their search yielded very few survivors. The devastation of that catastrophe... well, it was just too great. But today, you and your dogs can earn the chance to rescue others in dire need. So believe me, when I wish you all good luck"—she pressed a hand to her chest—"know that I mean it from the bottom of my heart."

A sudden lump of emotion lodged in Cat's throat. She swallowed hard and knelt to ruffle Halo's ears. "Okay, girl. Time to show 'em what you got."

SNAPSHOT OF A TASK FORCE

Earthquakes. Hurricanes. Tornadoes. Floods. Whenever and wherever these and other disasters happen, FEMA Urban Search and Rescue Task Forces arrive to provide emergency assistance. But what, exactly, are these elite squads?

There are twenty-eight Task Forces throughout the continental United States. Each has seventy members. For large-scale disasters like an earthquake, the Task Force is divided into two separate but identical units of thirty-five personnel each. That way, the units can take turns in the field to provide around-the-clock, uninterrupted services. If the disaster is smaller and more localized, then fewer members are deployed.

Members of the Task Forces are highly trained for all aspects of search and rescue missions. Doctors and physicians administer medical triage and treatment. Environmental specialists assess, handle, and remove hazardous materials. Structural engineers evaluate and stabilize unsafe structures. And of course, the canines and their human partners locate people trapped within collapsed buildings, buried and unseen beneath rubble, unconscious and unable to call or signal for help.

Each Task Force is ready to deploy within four to six hours of a disaster. Members are responsible for bringing their own personal gear and, in the case of canine units, gear for their dogs. In addition, a whopping 16,400 pieces of equipment are transported to the site. There are medical supplies to treat burn victims, stitch up wounds, and administer intravenous fluids. Cell phones, generators, and laptops to keep communications running smoothly. Jackhammers, saws, and construction vehicles to break up, cut through, and remove debris. And cots, bedding, food, and water, enough to sustain the Task Force for at least seventy-two hours.

Task Forces are truly amazing operations, peopled by amazingly dedicated women and men who choose to risk their own lives to save others.

"Okay, girl. Time to show 'em what you got."

The rules of the "game" were set: Halo had to find an unknown number of victims before the clock ran out. If she alerted Cat to anything other than a live victim, or if she failed to find all the victims, the "game" would be over—and Halo would fail.

Halo's tail swished through the dirt, kicking up a cloud of concrete dust that surrounded both her and Cat. She sneezed and wagged her tail again when Cat chuckled. Then Cat unsnapped her collar and stepped behind her. A second later, she felt Cat's hands resting on her haunches.

As light as it was, that touch electrified Halo. Adrenaline surged through her. Her hindquarters quivered in anticipation of Cat's first command.

"Ready?"

Halo answered with a low woof.

"Search!"

Halo raced across the open earth to the rubble pile. At its edge, she stopped short, eyes scanning for the best path up. When she found it—a flat slab here, a wooden pallet there, a half-pipe of concrete after that—she took tentative steps forward to test that the surfaces were stable.

Yes. It was safe to go on.

Her eyes and her ears and her cautious-but-surefooted tread were her allies in the move up and around the heap. In the early months of her training, she would have relied only on those senses. But that was then. Now her nose led the charge.

She scented the air, head turning this way and that. She smelled humans. Hard not to, there were so many around. Other dogs, too, some that had navigated the pile before her. And other smells, like plants and insects and dirt and food. It took willpower, but she ignored all these odors. The humans were clearly visible, and she was searching for those out of sight. The dogs, while interesting, didn't factor into the equation. As for the other smells, after an initial identification, she dismissed them completely.

Following a pattern that was part zigzag, part circular, she covered a small swath of the pile. Then suddenly—

Something. Something good. No—irresistible.

With an eager whine, she veered toward the scent. Somewhere down below, there was a warm body. A warm, furry body, like that of Rugger, her long-ago playmate who had once warned her away with a swipe of his clawed paw. Like the skinny feral cats on her home turf that teased her with spitting snarls before racing away, always just out of reach. As the scent grew stronger, her eagerness turned to obsession. And when she found the odor's source flowing from a small opening in the rock, her training flew out the window. She dug frantically at the hole, circling to get a better angle and reaching in as far as her front leg could go.

So close! So—

A soft April breeze had been wafting over the pile from the west. Now it switched direction, carrying with it a scent of human so ripe that it overpowered the smell of cat. Halo froze, then pulled her leg from the hole and lifted her nose into the scent cone.

This. This is what you're here for, her training whispered to her.

She left the hole and the cat below and once again let her nose guide her. Five steps and one careful hop down onto a tilted pallet, she came to a leaning wall of wooden planks. The intensely overwhelming human smell issued from between the tiny cracks.

Halo gave a sharp bark. Then another. She shoved her nose into the widest crack and inhaled again. And let out one more piercing bark followed by several others. This sustained, insistent signal, she had learned, would bring Cat to her. Her eyes and ears scanned the top of the pile for her human partner.

Nothing. Nothing. And then there she was, momentarily silhouetted against the sun. Halo barked again as Cat slowly and carefully picked her way to her side. Cat gazed at her for a moment, assessing. Then she smiled, pulled out a marker flag, and planted it in the planks.

A cat, Cat thought. *She almost failed because of a stupid cat. How ironic would that have been?*

When Halo had started digging at the first hole, Cat's stomach tightened into knots. And for good reason. To pass the Limited Access Rubble Pile test, Halo had to indicate her finds while out of Cat's sight and without any commands, verbal or hand signal, from Cat. Doing so proved that she could work independently and accurately without direction.

But Halo had stopped in full view of Cat. Because she didn't bark, Cat strongly suspected she wasn't pawing at a victim, but at something else. It was good she wasn't barking. That she continued to paw at the hole, though, wasn't so good. If Halo didn't abandon that spot and continue searching without Cat intervening…if she kept attacking the hole while time was running down... The knot in Cat's stomach had seized up even more tightly.

Luckily, after what seemed like forever, Halo had moved on. Cat was wondering what had caused her to go so crazy when a skinny feral cat suddenly squeezed its way out of the hole and darted away. Less than a minute later, Halo, now out of sight on the far side of the pile, started barking.

Cat tensed. Waiting. Listening.

Halo barked again. And then a third time. Cat let out a long breath and smiled.

Bingo. Still grinning, she started making her way up and over the rubble.

Twenty minutes later, the test ended. Unless she was mistaken—and as an evaluator herself, she didn't think she was—Halo had passed with two correct finds. It had been close, though. If Halo had barked at the cat to indicate a victim, if she hadn't moved on to the human scent...well, Cat didn't want to think about it. Besides, there was something more important to focus on: the Full Access Rubble Pile test.

Like the Limited Access, the Full Access Rubble Pile test was twenty minutes long, starting from when Cat released Halo. A maximum of six victims were used for the two tests combined; Halo had found two of the six in the limited pile, which meant there would be as many as four victims hidden throughout the rubble now. As before, Halo would be "naked," that is, wearing no collar or lead, as these could easily snag on debris and endanger the canine. The main difference was this time Cat would be part of the test, too, directing Halo with verbal and hand signals.

Under the watchful eyes of the three evaluators, Cat crouched behind Halo and gave the command to search. Halo streaked to the pile, stopped, twitched her nose through the air, and moved up to a small valley between two rocky rubble peaks. Cat followed, her heart hammering in her chest as her pride, love, and hope battled with her anxiety and stress. With the clock ticking, Halo needed to locate a victim soon.

Minutes passed without a single bark. Anxiety and stress took the upper hand in Cat's warring emotions.

"Halo, over!" she called, gesturing for her to move left.

Halo swung in the indicated direction, then hurried

forward when Cat gave that command. And then, a split second before Cat noticed it, Halo moved to a section of rubble. Halo sensed with her nose what Cat now saw with her experienced eyes: that section was just a little too tidy compared to the area surrounding it, as if someone had carefully repositioned a covering of planks and sheet metal over a hiding place. Halo stuffed her nose into a small opening, snuffled, then backed off and barked once, twice, three times.

Pride and love kicked stress and anxiety to the curb. Cat picked her way to Halo's side and whispered, "You're going to pass," in her perked-up triangle of an ear.

She marked the victim's spot and, with warm words of praise, gave Halo a toy to play with. After a few moments of listening to Halo squeak the squeaker, she took the toy back. With a firm command and wave of her hand, she sent her dog off to find another hidden volunteer.

Halo maneuvered over a boulder with a jagged crack down the middle and jumped onto a skinny plank. The plank looked stable enough until it wobbled, threatening to pitch Halo off balance and into the jagged debris below. Cat sucked in her breath, alarmed for her dog's safety.

She needn't have worried. Just as she had long ago on the backyard trampoline, Halo regained her footing without stumbling. She stepped off the plank and moved on. Across a pile of construction debris. Onto a mound of dirt-caked cement. Up a thick and rusted metal girder that thrust upward like a finger pointing at the sky.

Halo scaled the girder to its end. Ears forward and tail high, she lifted her nose into the air. Cat couldn't see her dog's coal-black nostrils, but she knew they were twitching. Sifting the odors drifting by on the breeze. Seeking the one that would send her onward toward her target. And she knew when that nose found what it sought because Halo suddenly leaped from the girder.

In that moment when she was airborne, her long front legs reaching forward and her powerful back legs and plume-like tail sailing behind, Halo looked just like a superhero to Cat.

No. Not a superhero, because those were just

make-believe, and Halo and canines like her were real. More than real—they were extraordinary.

"I'll tell you what you are." A small smile played on Cat's lips as she followed Halo with her eyes. "You're a superpower dog. And I can't wait to help you share those powers with the world."

VOLUNTEER OPPORTUNITY: SEARCH AND RESCUE "VICTIM"

For a truly up-close-and-personal look at canine search and rescue, nothing beats playing a victim. The bigger US&R training sites—like those in Virginia, Tennessee, Texas, California, and Florida, among others—often use outside volunteers during the FSA and CE tests. If your parent or guardian wants to look into these opportunities, they can do a quick online search to find which site is closest to where you live. Most have a website or social media account with contact info, so finding out about volunteer opportunities could be only an e-mail or post away.

You could also find a local youth service group with a history of providing volunteers to the US&R. There are two such programs, the Explorers and the Junior Cadets, in Miami-Dade, where Cat lives and works. Both are for teenagers between fourteen and eighteen years old with an interest in learning more about emergency response careers; the Explorers shadow and learn from members of the police department, while the Junior Cadets train with firefighters.

Before you talk to your guardian about signing on, though, you should first understand the role of the victim. Number one responsibility? Waiting in a cramped, filthy, hot space for a long stretch of time while a dog searches for you. Don't worry—you'll be provided with fresh cold water, earbuds, a radio, and the like, to make you as comfortable as possible. And other volunteers will check on you, too, to make sure you're okay! It's like a game of hide-and-seek, only instead of a friend coming to find you, it's a dog. The reward? The dog will practically burst with happiness at locating you. And if that isn't enough incentive, you're right there when the handler showers the dog with excited praise and pets.

"Whenever Halo finds her victim, I throw a huge

party," Cat says with a laugh. "A minutes-long, best-birthday-party-ever, wild celebration!"

And who knows? After a day in the rubble pile, you might just decide to explore the experience from the other side—and become a canine handler yourself in the future.

EPILOGUE

Halo was certified as a FEMA US&R canine on April 30, 2018. Another dog testing that same day did not pass, unfortunately. Perhaps he gave a false indication or missed finding a victim. Regardless, his handler will hopefully keep training him and try again in a few months. Because, like Cat, he knows what he's teaching his dog to do may one day mean the difference between a tearful reunion of a living, breathing survivor with his family... and an empty place at the dinner table because a life was lost to catastrophe.

Since her certification, Halo has continued training with Cat weekly, so when—and it's always *when*, never *if*—the next disaster hits, she'll be ready to serve. In the meantime, she's content to spend her free time playing soccer and bubbles with Lance, going on long runs with Pete, visiting her friends at the fire station and pet store, and reminding Cat with a guiding push of her paw that it's time for a belly scratch. Meanwhile, Cat recently matched four new FL-TF1 handlers with their first puppies—all yellow Labs because, as she knows so well, those are the easiest dogs to train. With lots of hard work and dedication, maybe in two years' time they'll be ready to join Halo on their first deployment.

In early September 2018, Cat got the call to deploy to the Carolinas with FL-TF1. The call was not unexpected; like most search and rescue personnel, she'd been monitoring the monstrous hurricane named Florence that was bearing down on the mid-Atlantic states. When the hurricane hit, she and her Task Force were in position and ready to help those in need.

Cat left one member of the team back home. "I didn't bring Halo," she said. "I knew other canines—older, more mature and experienced dogs—would be better at handling what we'd be dealing with. Plus, dogs aren't always needed because people tend to self-evacuate during hurricanes."

Instead of as a canine handler, Cat deployed as one of FL-TF1's search team managers. Hurricane Florence was predicted to cause catastrophic flooding, and Cat's role was to help ready the search efforts in the wake of those floods. Real-time maps of hard-hit areas were crucial to those efforts, so for nearly four weeks, Cat made sure her personnel had the best, most up-to-date street information possible.

After twenty-seven days in the Carolinas, Cat returned home to Miami and to Pete, Lance, and Halo. Halo greeted her with frenzied kisses and full-body wriggles that Cat returned with equal joy before falling into bed for much-needed sleep. But a mere thirty-six hours after unpacking, Cat was called up for search team manager duty again: this time to the Florida Panhandle on the Gulf Coast, where residents were bracing for Hurricane Michael.

Unlike Florence, which grew in size and strength over a number of days, Michael stunned many forecasters by erupting from a Category 1 to an immense Category 4 hurricane within forty-eight hours. It battered the Panhandle with drenching rain and sustained winds of more than 145 miles per hour. It ripped apart nearly every wooden structure in its path before heading inland and blowing itself out. "Toothpicks" was how Cat described the ruins. "Trees snapped like twigs. Unbelievable."

In the Carolinas, FL-TF1 had power, running water, dependable communication services, and decent indoor accommodations. In the heart of Panama City, where the team was stationed, Cat slept on a cot in a tent in the parking lot of a Home Depot. For the first two nights, before outdoor facilities were installed, she used bottles of water to shower.

"It wasn't great," she said, "but compared to what residents there were going through, it was paradise. I'd eventually return to my home. Those people had no homes to go back to. They lost *everything*. I can't imagine what that feels like."

Once again, Cat's main role was to put reliable maps in the hands of her searchers. "You want these guys to hit the ground running," she said. "Without these maps, they'll be running in place."

Cat spent a week and a half in Panama City. On October 19, she returned to Miami, exhausted both mentally and physically. "I slept ten, twelve hours every day for a week," she said.

And Halo?

"She cuddles me, hugs me," Cat said with a smile. "She's face-to-face with me when I wake up and pins my arms down to keep me from leaving the bed."

But after six weeks apart, it's time for Halo and Cat to return to their regular routine: to get back to the training facility and hone Halo's skills. Because the next disaster Cat deploys to—and there will be a next one, and no doubt many after that—Halo will be at her side. And Superpower Dog that she is, she'll be ready for whatever comes her way.

TIMELINE

- ★ **OCTOBER 2015**

    Halo is born.

- ★ **JANUARY 2016**

    Cat travels to Detroit, Michigan, and chooses Halo.

- ★ **FEBRUARY 2016**

    Halo's training begins.

- ★ **OCTOBER 2016**

    A training session at Fresh Kills Landfill with New York Task Force 1

- ★ **OCTOBER 2016**

    A training session in Jacksonville, Florida, with Florida Task Force 5

★ **NOVEMBER 2016**
   Another session in Jacksonville, Florida

★ **DECEMBER 2016**
   A training session in Virginia Beach with Virginia Task Force 2

★ **MARCH 2017**
   A training session in Memphis with Tennessee Task Force 1

★ **APRIL 2017**
   A training session in Gainesville, Georgia, with Georgia Task Force 1

★ **APRIL 2017**
   A training session in College Station, Texas, at Disaster City and TEEX

★ **OCTOBER 2017**
   Another session at Fresh Kills Landfill

★ **JANUARY 2018**
   Another session at TEEX

★ **APRIL 30, 2018**
   Halo is certified as a FEMA US&R canine.

SUPERPOWER DOG FACTS

DOGS AND TOYS

Dogs come in a wide variety of shapes and sizes, but they all need to play. Why do you think that is? Scientists have found that play helps to keep your dog physically and mentally healthy, builds a bond of trust and understanding with your dog, and helps your dog learn. Some dogs even find play to be more of a reward than food. Staff at animal shelters say dogs awaiting adoption may be offered two to three toys per day for comfort and play.

THE NOSE KNOWS

Human beings consider themselves to be pretty good at identifying smells. We can walk into the kitchen and know what's cooking. Dogs, with their smelling superpower, can do much more than this. Here are just some of the amazing things dogs can do with their noses:

- Track a lost child's scent trail through a busy city area forty-eight hours after the child was there.
- Find tiny quantities of drugs or explosives.
- Detect avalanche victims buried in snow.
- Help doctors to diagnose certain types of cancer.

Scientists are even training dogs to sniff out peanuts or latex products to protect people with severe allergies.

The cells that are receptive to odors are called olfactory sensory neurons. Not only do dogs have many more of these sensory cells than we do, they also have a proportionately larger part of their brain dedicated to processing this information than we do. And bloodhounds have millions more cells for odor detection than humans! Combine that with a brain capable of detecting a single odor hours after it was left behind, and you have a superpower.

WHAT'S THAT SOUND?

Ears are very important for helping dogs like Halo do their jobs. And unlike humans, dogs are able to raise, turn, tilt, and lower their ears. These abilities help them locate a sound source quickly, like a cry for help, which is a very important skill for working dogs.

For humans, the outer ear, or pinna, is shaped to help direct sound waves into the ear canal. For a dog with upright ears or "prick ears," such as Halo, this effect is even greater. Her larger ears do a better job of funneling the sound, and her ears are able to rotate toward the source of the sound because of eighteen special muscles on her head. Other dogs, such as bloodhounds, have floppy ears. These ears block distracting sounds, allowing the dogs to focus on smells.

TALKING WITH DOGS

As pack animals, dogs have lived and worked in groups since long before they began living alongside humans. To successfully survive in their team, they have a complex form of wordless communication. Working dogs need their human partners to understand what they're trying to tell them, so the dogs communicate through their ears, eyes, tail, and whole body. Here are some hints of what a dog might be saying, based on their position or actions:

What a dog might be saying	When you see them with their...
I'm ready to listen to you.	Ears facing forward. Tail held upright. Head up with back straight.
I'm hearing something somewhere.	Ears facing to the sides.
I'm afraid.	Tail tucked between the legs. Back hunched with head tucked down.
I'm ready to play.	Tail wagging. Chest down with elbows flat on the ground and rump up.

WHAT'S YOUR SUPERPOWER?

Think about the people in your life. Who would you go to for help with a tricky math problem? Who could suggest the best word for the story you're writing? Who will score the next goal in your soccer game?

Most people have a passion for certain subjects. We can quickly identify our own strengths or passions, and can often identify the strengths of others from the following list: word strong, number strong, music strong, art strong, sports strong, nature strong, people strong, and self strong.

Over the past centuries, different dog breeds became good at different things, and dogs continue to be selectively bred in part to excel in those certain skills. We could consider them to be smelling strong, hearing strong, caregiving strong, bravery strong, energetic strong, retrieving strong, herding strong, swimming strong, and snow strong.

What are your superpowers? What are your dog's? How can you use those strengths to make the world a better place?

The authors invite dog owners to visit superpowerdogs.com to share their dog's superpowers.

Fire captain Cat and Halo have developed a powerful bond.

Halo has always been curious, even as a puppy!

Like most puppies, Halo loves to play.

Cat tries to make training feel like a game for Halo and rewards her for doing well.

Cooling off, and having fun in the water, after a day of training.

Reporting for duty at the fire station where Cat works.

Halo and the humans around her have to prepare for many kinds of disasters.

Halo and Cat travel to Disaster City in Texas, a massive area designed to mimic a variety of real disasters.

One of America's biggest disaster training facilities is in College Station, Texas. Emergency response workers come from all over the world to train at Disaster City and the neighboring TEEX Brayton Fire Training Field. Here, firefighters observe a training scenario for an oil refinery blowout.

Halo will have to pass the biggest test of her life to become a certified disaster response dog. She's pictured here at the training site of New York Task Force 1 on Staten Island.

Halo and Cat with other members of Florida Task Force 1.